# psy'cho-
# a-nal'-y-sis:
### USES AND ABUSES

# psy'cho-
# a-nal'-y-sis:
## USES AND ABUSES

Lawrence J. Friedman, M.D.

*Paul S. Eriksson, Inc.*
*New York*

*To my wife, Marianne,
and my daughters,
Barbara and Lorraine*

# Foreword

There were many schools of psychology before Sigmund Freud and there are many today, but psychoanalysis designates only the specific discipline which was created by Freud: the theories of human development and behavior and the technique of therapy which were worked out by him, his co-workers and his followers. The word "psychoanalysis" was coined by Freud.

Psychoanalysis can be defined as:

(1) A theory of human psychology.
(2) A method for the study of the human mind.
(3) A technical tool for the treatment of a variety of emotional disturbances.

One of the cornerstones of psychoanalytic theory is the concept of the *Unconscious*. According to this concept, there are drives, desires, fantasies, attitudes, motivations in one part of the mind about which we know nothing. They are kept out of consciousness by a process called *Repression*. Yet these repressed, unconscious forces greatly influence our conscious attitudes and actions.

Psychoanalysis includes theories about the development and organization of the mind; the instinctual drives of the individual; the origin and growth of the conscience; the influences of the external environment; the importance of the family; the attitudes of society. It deals with the functioning of the individual in health, under stress and in illness. It attempts to discern and explain the success or failure of the individual in society, his ability or failure to establish satisfactory relationships with others, his character and character disturbances.

Before embarking on the following discussion of the theory and practice of psychoanalysis, a brief word about the history of the movement and about how psychoanalysts are trained may be helpful.

The history of psychoanalysis goes back approximately to the turn of the century. In 1900, Freud published "The Interpretation of Dreams," which to this day is considered the basic guide to understanding the significance of dreams and which encompasses the fundamental tenets of psychoanalysis. Although the book sold only a few copies in the first years after publication, it attracted the attention of a number of physicians, psychologists, lawyers, teachers, artists and writers. They formed the first group to study psychoanalysis. Some remained lifelong co-workers of Freud and outstanding scientific contributors to the field.

Others, among them some devoted early collaborators, dropped out when they became disturbed by some of Freud's revolutionary discoveries and when opposition to psychoanalysis, especially on the part of academic medicine, made it unpopular.

There is increasing acceptance as well as widespread opposition to psychoanalysis inside and outside the medical profession. The centuries-old, organic orientation of medicine, including psychiatry, is one of the important sources of opposition. The concept of the Unconscious is another. The idea that man is not master of all his thoughts and actions creates anxiety and is difficult for many to accept; yet this concept is the cornerstone of Freud's theories; without it, there is no science of psychoanalysis.

As time went on, more and more people wanted to study psychoanalysis, for a better understanding of human psychology and to use it for the treatment of certain emotional disturbances. With the increase in numbers, there was need for organization. The Viennese Psycho-Analytical Society was organized in 1902. Schools, journals and clinics were established, first on the continent of Europe and in England; later, in most other countries, including of course the United States. The first international congress took place in Salzburg, Austria, in 1908, and the International Psycho-Analytical Association was organized in 1910.

Because Freud was a Jew and because

psychoanalysis is the science of individual human psychology, it was violently opposed and its organizations ruthlessly destroyed on the continent of Europe during the Nazi era of derogating individual worth; and there are no psychoanalytic organizations in the Communist countries. The majority of the European psychoanalysts were forced to leave. Freud went to England and died in London, September 23, 1939, at the age of 83. Many came to the United States and, as a result, psychoanalysis achieved its greatest development in this country; unfortunately, also, its most flagrant and widespread abuses.

The Amercian Psychoanalytic Association was founded in 1911 and until about 1932, anybody who wanted to become a psychoanalyst could join the organization. There was very little organized training for some time. Most people who wanted to be trained as psychoanalysts went to Europe, to be analyzed by Freud or one of his co-workers and to study in their schools. Eventually, Psychoanalytic Institutes were organized in the United States and became the accredited centers for the training of psychoanalysts.

It was in 1938 that the American Psychoanalytic Association established the rule that only doctors of medicine would be accepted for training. This ruling has stirred controversy among analysts ever since, because there have been in the past and are today a number of outstanding, non-medical "lay analysts" who were trained prior to this ruling and who are still being trained in other countries.

Freud himself did not consider a medical education necessarily the best background for the training of an analyst. He thought that even though it offered the analyst much that is valuable, it also burdened him with much else that is irrelevant. He visualized an analytic college in which the training of analysts would include "elements from the mental sciences, from psychology, the history of civilization and sociology, as well as from anatomy, biology and the study of evolution" —and it would "omit from the curriculum anything which has no direct bearing upon the practice of analysis." ("Postcript to a Discussion on Lay Analysis, 1927.")

I might add that restricting psychoanalytic training to medical doctors eliminates a great number of creative, gifted, sensitive, psychologically-minded men, and especially women, because they are not attracted to long years of medical training. Due to their orientation and interest, many of them would not be accepted by a medical school even if they wanted to be. Yet some of the major contributions to the theory and practice of psychoanalysis have been and are still being made by some of the non-medical "lay analysts" both here and abroad. Best known among them is Anna Freud, who has neither an

M.D. nor a Ph.D. degree, yet who, after her father, Sigmund Freud, is the most important contributor to current psychoanalytic knowledge.

Training in the United States is available in the 20 Training Institutes approved by the American Psychoanalytic Association. During the past few years, the Association has approved for training some outstanding non-medical research workers in the behavioral sciences, so that they may use the tools of psychoanalysis in their own fields of endeavor. But training for the practice of psychoanalysis is limited to medical doctors.

After graduating from medical school, serving internship and residency in general psychiatry, it requires years of personal analysis, four to five years of theoretical courses and clinical work to become a psychoanalyst. Two years of practice, after graduation from a Training Institute, are also required before one becomes eligible for membership in the American Psychoanalytic Association. Personal analysis of the candidate is a basic requirement. Until he himself experiences the workings of his Unconscious, until he can understand himself, he will experience great difficulties in understanding his patients.

Unfortunately, in spite of the standards set by the American Psychoanalytic Association governing the training and conduct of accredited psychoanalysts, they are binding only on those who undergo training voluntarily at an approved

Psychoanalytic Institute. Yet psychoanalysis is not recognized either by the law or by the American Medical Association as a medical specialty. As a result, anyone within or outside the medical profession—without a day of psychoanalytic training, without even a high school education—can call himself a psychoanalyst and set up practice.

We may laugh at advertisements like "Psychoanalyst solves your marital and sexual problems, day or night"—or "Psychoanalysis and Palm-Reading"—but many of them attract lucrative practices. There are also too many well-meaning physicians, psychologists, social workers and others who, because psychoanalytic training is not legally required or is not available to them, believe that reading a few books qualifies them to practice psychoanalysis.

Psychoanalysis is a valuable tool for the investigation of the human mind and as a form of therapy for the treatment of certain emotional illnesses. It can be extremely helpful if used by trained experts; ineffective or even harmful in untrained hands.

The American Psychiatric Association has approximately 16,000 members, of whom only about 1,200 are at present trained and bona fide members of the American Psychoanalytic Association; and about the same number are currently undergoing training to become psychoanalysts. However, a basic knowledge of psychoanalytic theory is considered essential in the training of all psychiatrists—whether they eventually practice so-called psychoanalytically-oriented therapy, or some other form of psycho-therapy.

This is equally true for psychologists, social workers, nurses—for all who are involved in the treatment and management of emotionally disturbed people. It is valuable knowledge for physicians regardless of their specialty—not so that they may practice psychoanalysis but so that they may better understand human behavior and human conflicts, the varied reactions of their patients to illness, injury, medication or surgical intervention. Such understanding may prevent unnecessary emotional difficulties and influence the course of any illness.

Useful as psychoanalysis is as a therapeutic tool, its impact and value reach far beyond its medical application. *It is the only comprehensive theory of human psychology.* It has proven itself increasingly helpful to parents and teachers in the upbringing and education of children; to artists, judges, lawyers, anthropologists, historians and sociologists—to every science and discipline concerned with human behavior, human striving and human fate.

# Acknowledgments

I wish to express my appreciation to Dr. Hanna Fenichel and to Justice Shirley M. Hufstedler who first urged me to write this book, and to the many friends and colleagues whose advice, encouragement and helpful discussions contributed to its completion. My special thanks are due to Dr. Bertram D. Lewin for his valuable comments, as well as to Mrs. Sylvia Lewis for her expert editorial assistance on the several drafts.

I am grateful also to those who provided the forums over the years for the lectures upon which this book is based: Dr. Reuben Cordova, Director of Adult Education of the Beverly Hills Unified School District; Dr. Seymour Pollack, Director of the "Institute of Psychiatry and Law for the Judiciary" of the University of Southern California; Dr. George Savage of the Theater Arts Department of the University of California at Los Angeles; Donald Freed, Director of the Los Angeles Art Theater, among others.

Above all, my thanks are due to my patients, students, and the audiences from every walk of life who participated in my lectures and were my severest critics, insisting on clarifications and explanations of a complex subject in non-technical language understandable to any interested person.

# Table of Contents

xvi

## PART TWO

### THE PRACTICE OF PSYCHOANALYSIS

# psy'cho-
# a-nal'-y-sis:
## USES AND ABUSES

# PART ONE

# THE THEORY OF PSYCHOANALYSIS

# 1. Conscious—Preconscious—Unconscious

The following is a brief explanation of the three concepts used in psychoanalytic theory. The expression "subconscious"—so common in everyday speech—is not a psychoanalytic concept and the term is not used by psychoanalysts.

1. The *Conscious* is readily understood as that part of mental activity that we are fully aware of at any given time.

2. The *Preconscious* refers to thoughts and feelings which are not immediately available but which can be brought back to consciousness with a little effort. Like trying to remember a forgotten name: We may begin by saying, "It's on the tip of my tongue . . . let me see now . . . when I met him, I was at such-and-such a place . . . and so-and-so happened . . ." Then, all of a sudden, the forgotten name comes back to us.

3. The concept of the *Unconscious* is the foundation of psychoanalytic theory and practice. Psychoanalysts, just like other scientists, may have all kinds of theoretical differences. They may also differ in their therapeutic technique, like internists, for example, who do not necessarily

prescribe the same medicine for an illness, or sur-geons who do not necessarily use the same tech-nique when they perform surgery. But whatever disagreements exist among them, there is no dis-agreement about their acceptance of the existence and the effects of the Unconscious on human be-havior. To repeat: this concept holds that there are drives, desires, attitudes, motivations, fantasies in one part of the mind of which we are not aware. They are important because without our realizing it, they are responsible for many of our conscious feelings, thoughts, attitudes, actions, and they influence our relationships with others.

The Unconscious includes mental proc-esses of whose existence we are totally ignorant, as well as those we have been aware of at one time in our past but which, for many different reasons, we have pushed out of consciousness. They have been *repressed* and are now completely forgotten, like most things that happen to us during the early years of life. The repression of childhood memories (usually up to the age of five) is called "infantile amnesia." One of the goals of analysis is to lift the repression, to make unconscious con-flicts, drives, desires, etc., conscious, and to bring back to consciousness important forgotten memo-ries of childhood which affect our later develop-ment.

Freud's interest in the Unconscious dates back to the beginnings of his professional life when, as a neurologist, he became dissatisfied with the then-prevalent medical explanation of hysteria. The word hysteria derives from the Latin word for uterus. For this reason, it was generally believed that this puzzling phenomenon occurred only in women. Overlooked was the fact that the name (hysteria) was coined by men!

Freud found that men too suffered from this "female sickness." He and other neurologists of that period were at a loss to explain the peculiar convulsions or the complete paralysis of some part of the body which seemed to have no relation to any of the neurological patterns with which they were familiar. Realizing that there was no organic cause for these symptoms, Freud began to look elsewhere for explanations. This was the period during which he was interested in hypnotism. With its use, he was able to elicit the unconscious material which was at the root of the patient's hysterical symptoms. It was his work with hypnotism which originally convinced Freud of the existence of powerful unconscious forces which shape much of our lives.

There is no possible way to observe the Unconscious directly. To study its expressions, psychoanalysis uses the process of free association, the analysis of dreams, slips of the tongue, inexplicable actions, etc. The concept of free association developed out of Freud's realization that he learned more about his patients by listening to everything they said than by talking to them or asking questions. In effect, the analyst tells the patient to say everything that pops into his head, just as it pops into his head, even if he considers it nonsensical, unimportant, embarrassing or painful. This is very difficult to do at first because it is contrary to our entire upbringing, which emphasizes that we should think before we speak. One way to explain free association is to compare it with putting together a jigsaw puzzle. There are hundreds of pieces and none of them make sense alone; but slowly, patiently, we find a piece here which fits another piece there—and finally the pieces fall into place to make a whole.

Dreams are another important source for the study of the Unconscious. In our dreams, we can do things we don't even dare to fantasy about when awake, for fear we may actually act out our fantasies. But because we are immobilized while asleep and therefore do not act, our controls are loosened and we can express desires or find solutions for conflicts which are unacceptable in waking life.

In his observations of common, everyday slips of the tongue, Freud noted that people often reveal feelings and thoughts which are different from or even contrary to what they think they are saying. If you tell someone he has made a slip of the tongue, he will often deny having done so. A good example is a cartoon showing a married couple reading their newspapers. The wife, excited by the Travel Section, exclaims: "Darling, if *one of us* should die, *I'll* take a trip around the world." Or the story about the husband, away on a business trip, who writes to his wife: "Having a wonderful time, wish you were *her.*"

In addition to slips of the tongue, we all know people who constantly misplace or lose things; or who cut a finger every time they use a knife; or who are always having accidents; or are frequently cited for traffic violations. It is in studying why people do these things that we become aware that these actions are expressions of repressed, unconscious desires and conflicts which have broken through against our will.

Psychoanalysis investigates the Unconscious in order to understand human psychology and for purposes of therapy, so that it may find the answers to painful emotional symptoms for which there is no basis in reality, or to physical symptoms for which there is no medical explanation. It is one of the tasks of psychoanalysis to lift the repressions and bring out into the open the things which are disturbing us, making us ill.

Contrary to one of the greatest misconceptions of all time, that what we don't know won't hurt us, *it is precisely the things that we do not know about ourselves which are responsible for many of our emotional disturbances.* The skeleton in the closet is frightening only so long as the door remains closed, so long as we don't dare to look at it.

9

## 2. Instinctual Drives—Sexual Development

An instinctual drive is an inner need seeking satisfaction. It is a continuous need, which disappears only when it is satisfied—just as hunger disappears after eating, or sexual desire after an orgasm. The two major instinctual drives which dominate human behavior are the libidinal drive and the aggressive drive. The libidinal drive includes not only the sexual drive but all the emotions and needs which are encompassed in the broader meaning of the word love.

For centuries it was believed that the first signs of sexuality appeared only at puberty. The general public, including the medical profession, reacted with disbelief, shock, even scorn when Freud pointed out that this was a fallacy and offered his theory of infantile sexuality. Even though expressions of infantile sexuality are all around us for anyone to see, it has remained a subject of controversy and a source of opposition to psychoanalysis to this day.

People in our civilization have difficulty accepting the fact that there are expressions of the developing sexual drive in human beings from

10

the earliest beginnings. Most people interpret the word sexual only in terms of adult sexuality. But just as the physical sexual organs exist from the beginning of life, so does the drive for sexual activities and satisfaction. Both develop within the individual until they reach the stage of adult functioning. This is as true for sexuality as it is for any other function. They all have beginnings which are not identical with the end results; but without these beginnings, the end results could not come about.

Freud schematically divided sexual development into four phases: the oral phase, centering around the activities of the mouth; the anal phase, connected with the anus and elimination; the phallic phase, when the interest of the child turns to the sexual organs; and finally, the genital phase during puberty, leading to sexual maturity and to adult sexual functioning.

Each of the four phases—occurring during the growth of the individual—is characteristic of a certain age. It must be understood, however, that this does not mean that one phase starts at birth; another at age two; another at age three, etc., but that a continuous developmental process is involved. Each succeeding phase carries with it elements of the preceding phase and, as it evolves, takes on characteristics which are predominant at certain age levels. Furthermore, there are individual variations. Some children develop more

11

quickly, some more slowly—depending on their given potential, the external environment, and the attitudes of the important figures in their lives from the day they are born.

Actually, what we call sexual play in adult sexual behavior includes every one of the phases which are part of sexual development throughout the first years of life. We use the mouth . . . the hands . . . we look . . . we exhibit . . . we touch . . . smell . . . and so on. All this is part of adult sexuality. Any person who is unable to enjoy sexual play, or who has to avoid it altogether because it represents prohibited, anxiety-laden, guilt-laden activities in his sexual development during childhood—is not capable of full and satisfactory adult sexuality.

To summarize, then: When we speak of infantile sexuality, we do not mean adult sexuality. We refer to the steps which, if unimpeded, eventually evolve into adult sexuality. This is true for every human function, sexual or otherwise. Each goes through a lengthy, difficult evolution from the day we are born until we finally develop into functioning, adult human beings.

## 3. The Oral Phase

A newborn infant experiences his first pleasurable sensations with his mouth. After he is born and loses his physical connection with the mother's body, he uses his mouth to suck for food; it is the only way for him to stay alive. This need is associated with pleasurable sensations involving the mouth.

Nature has seen to it that all the activities of the human body which are necessary to maintain life and to perpetuate the race are endowed with pleasurable sensations. If, for any reason, there is no pleasure connected with these activities, emotional or physical disturbances inevitably arise.

Whether the infant feeds from the breast or the bottle, he sucks food into his mouth. However, we observe that the sucking is not just a mode of eating; he enjoys doing it even when he is not eating. Before this was recognized, people believed that children sucked their thumbs only because they were hungry. This is not true at all. The infant may suck his thumb when he is hungry, but he will also do it when he is not. Thumb-sucking is independent of eating. It is a pleasurable, perfectly normal activity, an expression of infantile sexuality, a phase in the development toward adult sexuality.

The very first relationship in the early weeks and months of an infant's life (which is limited exclusively to the mother or mother substitute) will influence his development and capacity for future relationships, not only sexually but in many ways. Whether a child at this stage enjoys eating, or becomes disgusted because he is forced and overfed, or frustrated because he is underfed, will affect the foundation laid for further development.

It is not only the quantity and quality of food that count but also by whom and how it is given. One of the misconceptions of every affluent society is that if one gives a child all the milk, all the vitamins, all the physical necessities he requires, the job is done. Nothing could be further from the truth. An infant needs much more than that. He needs *mothering*. Feeding is, in a manner of speaking, a love relationship. The infant needs a loving mother who cuddles and holds him during his feedings, and enjoys doing it. This is as important as the food itself.

Observation of children in orphanages reveals that prolonged separation from the mother (without an adequate substitute) —especially during the first year of life—creates serious emotional and physical difficulties, even if all the right food is available; even in the cleanest and most hygienic surroundings. Many later disturbances can be traced back to the oral phase.

## 4. The Anal Phase

Following the preoccupation with the activities and pleasures of the mouth, the infant's interest turns to the functions and organs of elimination, especially the anus. We call this the anal phase. Generally this occurs in the second year and reaches its height between the ages of two and three.

Even though their bowel movements remain a lifelong preoccupation of most people, the idea that anality is a phase in the sexual development of human beings is hard for them to accept, so many social prohibitions are involved. Yet all we have to do is to observe infants to recognize their intense interest in their bowel functions and all the activities connnected with the anus. In addition to the pleasurable sensations involved, the anus also arouses particular curiosity because it is one of the parts of the body we cannot see. Other animals can see their anuses; only humans cannot.

Only if we refuse to face facts is it possible to overlook the absorption and pleasure children find in the functions and productions of the anus. It is a major event in the process of growth when a child discovers the value of his feces as an important part of his body which are his to give or withhold. This is the first exchange value human beings possess. It can be traded for love. It can be used to express one's own will. It marks a significant step toward independence. Frequently it becomes the battleground between the child and the adult world.

There is nothing new about this. During the Middle Ages alchemists were convinced that if they could only find the formula, they could make gold out of feces. Equating feces with gold expresses symbolically the child's overvaluation of this precious production of his body. He is reinforced in his feeling by the intense reactions of his mother to this activity. Think what goes on during toilet-training! There is hardly an adult in the child's environment who is not preoccupied with the color, consistency, shape, quantity, size, smell, frequency and regularity of the child's bowel movements.

This is the phase during which a child learns that to refuse to produce on demand and to say directly, "I won't," is dangerous. Mother will be angry, she may punish him, he may lose her love. But there is a way out. Presently, he learns that he can refuse even more effectively by being good. The new slogan is, "I would love to, but I can't." He will sit on the potty, slide around after you from room to room, and still nothing happens. Nevertheless, Mother insists, society insists, and the infant learns to bargain. He learns to exploit the innumerable ways by which he is seduced, bribed or forced to give up his precious treasure. This is the period out of which many of the prevalent character traits in our society develop. Some children will become independent individuals, able to work well without resentment, even with pleasure. Others will start out with big promises, big intentions, big plans, and nothing will ever come of them. Some will be capable of accepting responsibilities, others will reject or rebel against them or will postpone all action until the last moment, like children jumping up and down on one foot to postpone going to the toilet until it is absolutely unavoidable or until it is too late.

This is the period during which the child struggles for independence and comes into conflict with the outer world. Before this, children are quite helpless. It is relatively easy and natural for mothers to take care of helpless infants; the feeling of being needed is a constant source of satisfaction, even pleasure. The picture changes radically when the struggle for independence begins. During this phase, children are stubborn, ornery, say "no" to everything. Even if you offer a piece of candy which the child wants, he says "no." He insists on his own will, as if to say: "I won't . . . you can't make me . . . I'll do what *I* want."

The anal character is the most predominant character in our society. It reveals itself in many ways. There are the generous and the stingy; the meticulous collectors and the spendthrifts; the orderly and the disorderly who make a mess of everything.

To a child, there is nothing dirty or disgusting about his feces. He enjoys playing with them, smelling them; they are a valuable production of his own body, a source of pleasure and power. Mother, the family, society, force the child to give up this pleasure. He does give it up. He learns to play with mud pies, the deodorized substitute for feces. Of course, mothers frequently react as though the mud is just as "dirty" as the feces. So mud is replaced by clay. Clay is socially acceptable and parents buy it by the ton. It is almost identical with the original, in color, form, consistency.

As time goes on, children move further and further away from the feces. They progress to the sandbox, the dehydrated substitute. But how much more fun it is to play in the wet sand at the beach! To dig deep holes, build forms and figures! Even parents join in the fun. Older children learn to finger-paint. Grown men smoke pipes, combining adult orality by sucking and biting their pipes, with anality by constantly cleaning them until their fingers are all brown and smelly. Women progress to more delicate substitutes—deodorants, nice-smelling soaps and perfumes.

Whether one creates a beautiful painting or just smears a canvas depends on his innate talent. Without talent, the production will resemble the original smearing. Obviously, there are more people who can smear than create. Their productions, misnamed art, are frequently inferior to those of nursery-school children yet they fill galleries. Psychoanalysis does not claim to know just how creative talent originates, but it does know a good deal about creative activity—what promotes it and what interferes with it.

Even a gifted, productive artist can experience difficulties and become unable to work if shame, anxiety and guilt about early anal activities are remobilized. I knew one such who could not touch a canvas for years. With palette in hand, he would stand in front of a clean white canvas each morning . . . paralyzed, panic-stricken, unable to touch or soil its immaculate surface. It took years before he could function again. Eventually, as his anxiety decreased, he developed a method which permitted him to paint again. First he mixed a bucketful of dirty brown paint—just a thin liquid—and splashed it over the canvas. Now the canvas was no longer white, but dirty. By yielding to his desire to soil it, he could paint again, go on to create something beautiful.

To avoid misunderstanding, let me emphasize that psychoanalysis does not equate the artistic creation of a painter with a child's pleasure in smearing. It only points to the common origin. Some, who are gifted, may develop into fine painters. Others, with or without talent, will turn everything they touch into something dirty and destructive—whether it be a canvas, a book, an idea, or their very lives.

Whether the end result will be ugly or beautiful will depend on their innate abilities, the experiences with the environment, and the attitudes of the important adults toward the activities of the child during the early years of development. One may become an artist, a statistician, a collector of beautiful and valuable items, or a collector of worthless objects or knowledge. Probably a majority of us collect worthless items like paper bags, empty jars, old newspapers. We do not realize how big these collections are until we sell a house or move to another apartment and have to clean out the garage or empty the overflowing shelves. Even when faced with the necessity, it is difficult to part with these treasures.

Collectors of valuable items like to show them off, to be admired and praised for them, just like the infant who proudly presents his feces to his mother for her recognition and approval. How disappointing and painful if the mother reacts with nothing but disgust, if his production

21

is considered just dirty, just something to get rid of!

The preoccupation with bowel movements in our society is almost incredible. It reaches into every phase of life, in health and in illness. Think how large a proportion of commercial advertising is devoted to the subject. And why not? The moment anyone has a headache, backache, is tired, has a fever or a cold, sore throat, pneumonia, muscle pain, loss of appetite, a hangover—the first question, from family and friends, even from doctors, is: "When did you move your bowels?" This is followed by every latest nostrum medicine can conjure up for you to swallow or put into the rectum in the form of pills, capsules, liquids, oils, enemas high and low, soap sticks, irritating suppositories of every imaginable size, shape and color. Why? There is no rational explanation. As a matter of fact, the feverish, often drastic methods employed to cajole a movement out of an unwilling bowel may often do more harm than good.

Mothers, grandmothers, doctors and nurses set the standard for the amount, size, shape and consistency by refusing to accept the fact that children and adults have their own quite individual styles. They will produce short ones, long ones, round ones or hard ones. Some people move their bowels every day with solemn ceremony. Others pay no attention to when and how. Just because there are differences, does not make one style healthy and the other sick. Also associated with anal activities is the almost delusional preoccupation in our society with dirt and all manner of body odors.

Money can be just money, a reality to be dealt with in daily life. But if that were all, we would all deal with money in the same way. Instead, one can hardly find two people with the same attitude toward money. The wide variance in adult attitudes is directly connected with their experiences during infancy with the "first money in the bank," the feces. Some use it to express power; others to give or withhold love. Some brag about it, some are secretive. Some will talk with the greatest ease about their intimate sexual activities but are deeply embarrassed to talk about money. "Money is dirty." Why? What makes it "dirty"? They feel it is dirty because it symbolizes the feces and evokes the same feelings and conflicts they experienced during the anal phase.

Many people have all kinds of difficulties in dealing with cash. They find it relatively easy to buy on a charge account; even writing a check is not too difficult, it's only a promise, a piece of paper. But cash! That's something else again. How we hang on to it, how we hate to part with it! The smaller the amount, the greater the problem, because the smaller the reality value, the closer it comes to the symbolic meaning. For many, it is easier to pay out a ten-dollar-bill than to put a penny in a parking meter. They will drive around for blocks looking for one showing a few minutes of unexpired time. Or how about the people who will spend fifteen or twenty dollars for dinner without hesitation, but go through tortures trying to decide how much to tip? Or those who sneak away from the drugstore counter after eating, when the waitress isn't looking, so they won't have to leave a dime?

Our daily language is full of expressions equating money with feces. A good bowel movement makes one "feel like a million dollars."—"That man is filthy rich."—And the language of poker players is pure anality.

## 5. The Phallic Phase

Just as, during the anal phase, interest shifts from the mouth to the anus, so during the phallic phase the genitals become the center of interest. The little boy's interest and preoccupation with his penis are easier to observe than the genital activities of the little girl. The little boy shares his interest with all men, women and children in both primitive and civilized societies. The importance and value of this "handy little gadget" have been emphasized and over-emphasized throughout human history.

The little boy discovers that touching and playing with his penis, previously regarded as primarily an organ to urinate with, is very pleasurable. So he experiments and manipulates it. This we call masturbation. The little girl's masturbatory activities center around stimulation of the clitoris.

Masturbation is a perfectly normal activity for all children at this stage. They do not need any encouragement or instruction, and the less we interfere with it, the fewer problems we create for ourselves and for the children. However, misconceptions and prejudices about masturbation are still so widespread that when communicated to the child they can seriously interfere with the future course of his sexual development. These superstitions are handed down from generation to generation, perpetuating guilt, anxiety, feelings of worthlessness. Among the most prevalent are that masturbation drains vital body substances and causes physical weakness, mental weakness, softening of the brain, insanity, blindness, anemia, skin diseases . . . that it ruins the penis and causes impotence . . . that it results in homosexuality . . . that it is a perversion practiced only by "degenerates." Ipso facto, a child who masturbates is a "degenerate."

Nor are these fantastic notions confined to the layman alone. Even today, studies reveal that quite a few practicing physicians in this country still believe that many mental illnesses are caused by masturbation. And to top it all, many religious sects condemn it as a sin. As long as people continue to live with these superstitions, they will try to interfere with masturbation in every possible way. Parents try to divert children with persuasion, bribery, threats, physical restraints and punishment. One of the mildest approaches is, "Keep your hands over the blanket"—a reversal from earlier times when the child wanted to suck his thumb and was ordered to "keep your hands under the blanket."

Coinciding with their increasing interest in the genitals, children experience intense sexual curiosity during the phallic phase. Looking and exhibiting are very conspicuous. They ask many questions and sooner or later, they get answers—right ones or wrong ones. If they are told honestly that the baby comes from inside the mother, they want to know how it comes out and how it got there. They want to know what it has to do with the penis and why there are differences between male and female genitals.

This is the period during which correct or incorrect handling of sexual curiosity can either minimize or increase anxiety about infantile sexual activity, with its resultant effects on adult sexuality. What is more, sexual curiosity during this phase is accompanied by a growing curiosity about everything. Curiosity is the basis for the learning process. The attitude of the adults toward a child's sexual curiosity, therefore, can promote or interfere with the learning process in general. A secretive, prohibiting, punishing attitude can convince a child that curiosity, inquiry, knowledge are dangerous. This may result in a learning inhibition. . . as if the child were saying to himself: "I must not ask questions . . . I must know only what I am told. What I am not told, I must not know. I'd better deny, forget or conceal whatever I do know, because I'm not supposed to know."

We live in a presumably enlightened society, yet neither moon rockets, nor Telstar, nor any of the other miraculous technical achievements of our age have influenced our ancient anxieties, shame, guilt and unrealistic, distorted attitudes toward sexual desires and activities. Attitudes range from outright condemnation to conditional acceptance—from hypocritical morality to pseudo-sophistication. Too many consider sex "dirty" and so they make it dirty and because of our double standard, this degrading of sexuality automatically degrades woman. She becomes, not the attractive, exciting, equal sexual partner but a "broad"—"a piece of ass." It is food for thought that the picture of a beautiful human body is considered pornography while we sing praises to the "Body By Fisher!"

With the exception of a minority who are totally inhibited for one reason or another, all human beings crave sexual activity and practice it, whether with more or less pleasure or satisfaction. Those who experience the greatest guilt and the least satisfaction are the first to righteously condemn all sexuality and those who enjoy it. The greater the condemnation, prohibition and punishment, the greater the preoccupation with sex and the more it permeates all phases of life.

We use it seductively to sell deodorants, alcohol, cigarettes, toilet paper; to lure young and old to sexy movies, nightclubs, "topless" bars, burlesque shows; to sell pronographic literature; to promote gambling and prostitution. If sexual seduction is used for commercial advertising purposes, the seducer is rewarded with wealth and respectability. If it is used for "illegitimate" seduction, like sexual stimulation, pleasure or activity, we condemn the seduced and prosecute the seducer. We make rules about what constitutes "normal" sexuality—which sexual practices are permissible—and declare all deviations to be "abnormal"—"unnatural"—"criminal." We turn with special vengeance on the "perversions" which resemble the normal developmental phases of infantile sexuality.

Yet it is psychoanalysis which is accused of being overly preoccupied with sex! Certainly psychoanalysis would like to help bring about a better understanding among children and adults of the true nature and function of sex in human life. But education toward a healthy and responsible attitude toward sex is neglected, resisted or condemned by all too many parents, school boards, the law. Even by the medical schools, many of which teach only the anatomy, physiology and pathology of the sexual organs but nothing about sexual activity, about either normal or pathological sexual behavior. Yet people automatically turn to their doctors for help with their sexual problems and difficulties.

# 6. The Oedipus Complex

Derived from Sophocles' immortal version of the Greek legend about Oedipus, King of Thebes, Freud gave the name of Oedipus complex to his discovery of the most crucial conflict which every human being undergoes in the course of his early development. Briefly, the story about Oedipus goes as follows:

Separated from his parents in infancy, Oedipus returns to Thebes as an adult and, ignorant of their identity, unwittingly kills his father, the king, and marries his mother, the queen. Years later, when he learns the truth, his despair leads him to blind himself, give up his kingdom and, driven by guilt, wander the earth, an abandoned, homeless outcast.

Where did this myth spring from? It could only have sprung from the depths of the Unconscious of the human mind, symbolizing desires and conflicts experienced universally during early childhood, even though generally they are buried in the Unconscious. The taboo against incest is as old as time—a prohibition enforced throughout human history by punishments often more severe than for any other crime. Laws exist to prohibit those impulses which human beings want to indulge and would indulge if they were not afraid of punishment. There are no laws forbidding things people don't want to do anyway.

Psychoanalysis affirms that during the phallic-Oedipal phase, every little boy experiences desires, fears, conflicts related to those expressed with poetic license in the Oedipus legend. His new-found pleasure in masturbating is bound up with unconscious sexual fantasies centering on his mother and destructive feelings toward his father, the hated and powerful rival for his mother's love. With certain modifications, the little girl follows a similar path. Therefore, psychoanalysis concludes that during this phase all children experience sexual desires toward the parent of the opposite sex and want to eliminate the parent of the same sex. Even though in most cases this is experienced only as unconscious conflict, expressions of these feelings are sometimes quite open. A little boy who is not afraid will tell his father frankly that when he grows up and the father is dead, he will marry Mommy. At the same time, he reveals his rivalry, anger, even physical violence against the father in many other ways.

The Oedipal phase of development is a difficult period for the boy under any and all circumstances. If the father is cruel, punishing, the boy becomes even more terrified of his desires. If instead, the father is always kind and understanding, the boy feels even more guilty about his angry, destructive feelings toward him. The conflict is further complicated because he not only hates and resents his father during this period, but also loves him and wants to be loved by him. The inevitable consequences of this ambivalent conflict are that his destructive fantasies toward the beloved father provoke strong feelings of guilt and fear of retaliatory punishment.

At about this time, too, the boy becomes increasingly aware of the fact that girls do not have a penis. He believes that it was lost or taken away from them. He fears that he will also be punished by having his penis, the organ of so much pleasure, cut off or taken away. This fear is called *castration anxiety,* which shows itself in many ways. A boy at this stage may have a horror of injury and may panic if told he must get a haircut or if he so much as cuts his finger. Later on, castration anxiety may be the cause of a man's fear of women—especially aggressive, so-called castrating women. A soldier in combat may remove his helmet to cover his genitals and will explain: "If I get shot in the head, I'll die. To live without my penis would be worse than death."

The Oedipus complex reaches its height during the fifth year. Normally, at that point, the boy, filled with castration anxiety for his "bad" feelings, realizing that he is too small

and weak to compete with his powerful father—
all the while needing and loving him as well as
hating him—begins to move away from his fixation on the mother and identifies with the father.
So, in the normal course, the Oedipus complex
is resolved and the door opened on the road to
adult manhood. The love for the mother becomes
*desexualized* and, by losing its sexual meaning,
becomes the basis for a satisfactory adult relationship between mother and son and for the son's
ability to turn his sexual interest toward other
women.

Difficult as all this is for boys, it is even
more so for girls. A boy starts out by desiring his
mother, eventually gives her up, and finally ends
by loving another woman. The little girl starts
out from the same point, but her maturation must
go through an even more complicated development. In her case, too, the mother is the first love
and she wants her all to herself, just as the boy
does. During the phallic-Oedipal phase, when she
becomes acutely aware that the boy has a penis and
she does not, she begins to hate her mother for
not having given her one. She suffers from intense
penis envy and in her disappointment turns to her
father, who has a penis and who, in her sexual
fantasies, will give it to her by making her pregnant, giving her a baby. Now the mother becomes
the intruder, the hated rival she wants to
eliminate.

In the course of a normal resolution of the Oedipus complex in the little girl's case, she eventually gives up her sexual desires for the father and, as if compensating for the lack of a penis by a foreknowledge that she will some day be a mother herself and create babies, she again turns to the mother and identifies with her. This renewed identification is a prerequisite for the achievement of adult womanhood and the ability to love a man other than her father, and to herself become a wife and mother. (See also the chapter entitled "Female Sexuality and Masculine Bias.")

Vicissitudes in the resolution of the Oedipus complex can result in serious emotional difficulties in adult life. They can be the cause of severe guilt and anxiety; the source of crippling sexual problems for both men and women; the inability to establish or maintain satisfactory relations with the opposite sex.

The role of the Oedipus complex in both healthy and pathological development is crucial. Its successful resolution is a prerequisite for mature functioning, not only sexually but in every other respect as well. A man who remains permanently attached to the mother of his childhood fantasies will not be able to establish a mature relationship with another woman. If he cannot resolve his original competitiveness with his father, competition will represent danger to him all his life. He may be able and industrious, but he will be afraid to succeed, will have a need always to defeat himself. More people break down who are on the verge of success, or are already successful, than those who are failures from the start. Like the outstanding bankruptcy lawyer who can deal with everyone's bankruptcy but his own; the athlete who always comes in second; the eternal vice president; the girl who is always a bridesmaid, never a bride.

Far more crippling even than these disabilities is what happens when the destructive fantasies of children toward their parents are encouraged and exploited, as they were in Germany and Italy during the time of Hitler and Mussolini. Children were ordered to report to their teachers or leaders any criticisms of the regime they heard at home and were rewarded for doing so. Imagine what happens to a child who grows up knowing that willingly or carelessly he may have contributed to the torture or death of a parent. Many children did just this and, from all we know about human development, it can have devastating consequences for generations to come.

## 7. Latency—Puberty—Adolescence

At the end of the stormy phallic-Oedipal phase, comes a period of relative peace, the latency period. The conflicts of the earlier years are forgotten, repressed. This is when children normally, almost abruptly, begin behaving like little angels. They love Mommy and Daddy and even show tolerance toward brothers, sisters, friends. Freed temporarily from the pressures of their internal conflicts, their interests turn to the outside world.

Ideally, this is when formal schooling should begin, when they are most receptive to learning not only the three R's but the need for accepting the rules and restrictions of the larger community they are entering. How quickly children will adjust will depend partly on their teachers and their schools, but mainly on their upbringing during the turbulent pre-school years. Children who have never been taught to accept discipline in the home will of course have a more difficult time.

The relative peace of the latency period comes to an abrupt end with the beginning of puberty. The turmoil of the phallic-Oedipal phase, left behind around the age of five, is re-activated. Sexual fantasies and desires are re-awakened, but with a difference. Earlier, all the child could do was to wish, to fantasy and mastur-bate. At puberty, however, even though masturba-tion once again becomes the major sexual activity, he is physically capable of heterosexual activity and satisfaction.

In primitive cultures this is taken for granted, but for many reasons our complex society demands that such activity be postponed long be-yond the age of sexual maturation. There are youngsters who do not find it too difficult to abide by this restriction but the majority ignore it or are unable to control it in spite of their guilt, anxiety and good intentions. All too often the consequences are tragic. The widespread use of alcohol and stimulants among young teenagers contributes greatly to the difficulties.

Obviously, there are no easy solutions to the sexual dilemmas of our adolescents, any more than to the problems of violence, delinquency, and the other ills of our world. But adequate and healthy sex education would help them to under-stand and accept the necessity for postponing het-erosexual gratification, for which they are emo-tionally unprepared. By the time they reach pu-berty, young people should have been taught about every aspect of sexuality—not only about the anatomy and physiology of the sex organs but about the emotional, social and legal responsibilities demanded by society of the sexually and emotionally mature adult.

Instead, as we all know, sex education is rejected on religious, moral, legal and many other grounds, dictated by centuries of superstition, fear, shame and guilt. The result is ignorance—the breeding ground for emotional and physical illness —the most fertile soil for untold human misery, impotence, frigidity, every kind of sexual problem in and outside of marriage.

Little children are "too young to be told"—the true facts, that is, but not too young to be indoctrinated with fears and distortions by parents, the church and every medium of communication and entertainment. Teenagers are "too young for explanations"—but not too young to be infected with venereal diseases in alarmingly increasing numbers. Or to become pregnant and be exposed to exploitation by illegal and unscrupulous abortionists who can endanger their health, their future, their very lives. Or to fill adoption agencies and orphanages with infants they don't want and couldn't care for.

This is the price we pay for our hypocritical and contradictory attitudes, alternating between pseudo-sophistication, talk of "sexual freedom," exploitation, constant stimulation and outright condemnation.

One important factor which is lost sight

of is that from the early years till the late teens, girls mature earlier than boys, physically, sexually, emotionally and intellectually. In the graduating class of a junior high school many look more like mothers with their sons than like contemporaries. Unfortunately these differences are ignored, especially in education. In my opinion, it is unwise to raise children in coeducational schools during the formative years, especially during puberty. In these schools, boys and girls are forced from the start to compete with one another. Boys, sensing their disadvantage, compete by depreciating learning and by rebellious, undisciplined behavior. What is more, as they mature, they are constantly exposed to sexual stimulation by their physically more mature classmates, and sexual excitement does not encourage concentration on mathematics! The only class where the boys and girls are separated is the gym class, the one in which the boys might at least be able to display their greater physical skills.

The battle of the sexes is as old as mankind and we encourage it by raising boys and girls to compete with each other on unequal terms. A further complication is the fact that the majority of teachers, especially in the grade schools, are women, aggravating the boys' fear and resentment of female authority.

The consequences are far-reaching in our culture, where the role of the father in the upbringing of children is not very influential. It would be highly desirable to have more men teachers, especially for the boys. Boys need fathers and father-figures with whom to identify. They need men to look up to during this phase of development. The more they are deprived of their influence, the more they lose confidence in their own masculinity and tend to substitute violence for masculinity.

Puberty and adolescence are stormy periods to live through. It is not easy to deal with the pressures of instinctual desires and the internalized and external prohibitions against them. Adolescents not only rebel against the restrictions imposed on them by parents, teachers, society. They want to live by their own rules. At the same time, even though they clamor for unlimited freedom, they feel abandoned if they have to carry the burden of responsibility for all their actions themselves. This, above all, is a time when they need understanding and wise judgment on the part of parents and all the important adults in their lives. Although they may deny it, they know inwardly that they need guidance and the establishment of some limits, some controls on their behavior.

The adolescent turbulence continues until the late teens when, just as during the latency period, it dies down. At 17 or 18, the youngsters are usually more mature than we might expect. This is when most of them go out into the adult world, either to work or to college. Those who were fortunate enough to live through this rebellious phase in an understanding environment, will do well. Those who experienced no controls, or were too severely restricted, will be among the first to run into difficulties when they leave home.

## 8. The Aggressive Drive

The concept of Aggression is widely misconstrued, not only by the general public but by many experts in the field of human relations as well. Most people associate it exclusively with violence and destructiveness. The reason for this is clear enough. For many years it was believed that we were all born quite blank emotionally, "just little bundles from heaven." Displays of anger, destructiveness, violence were interpreted as reactions to reality frustrations—to interference with the satisfaction of needs such as hunger, sexual pleasure, or other needs.

This is what we were told by the church, the law, sociology, psychiatry, by all those who had anything to do with understanding and influencing human behavior. Even today there are students of the behavioral sciences who believe that anger is a reaction to frustration only; that violence is the result of unfavorable social conditions. Certainly frustration and oppressive social conditions can elicit destructive expressions of aggression but they do not constitute its basic source. To believe that they do is naive. It tells us no more about aggression than an electric spark from a defective fuse tells us about electricity. It ignores everything we have learned about the Unconscious. What is more, even the most superficial observation of any individual or of society contradicts any such assumption.

Psychoanalysis does not claim to have all the answers but believes today that aggression is one of the drives inherent in human nature. We may conceive of aggression as energy, a powerful force which can be used for either constructive or destructive purposes. Freud once compared it to a river flowing peacefully along, its great energy potential hidden, unrealized, until it is blocked in its course or swollen by torrential rain, when it overflows its boundaries and becomes a raging, violent force, destroying everything in its path.

By building dams, we can harness this great energy to turn the wheels of generators, transforming it into electricity. We do not see the tremendous force of electricity, either, just by looking at electric wires, but only if it is blocked or utilized. We cannot even imagine life today without the benefits of electricity, yet it, too, can be an instrument of destruction—to wit, the electric chair. The cattle prodder and the flashlight use the same batteries.

Similarly, we can use aggressive energy. The question is what do we use it for—pleasure or pain—life or death. It requires aggressive energy to move our muscles, to walk, to eat, to compete in sports, to make love, to work. Or we can use it to torture, kill, destroy. It takes the same energy to kiss or to bite, to caress or to scratch, to take a step or to kick.

Just as we are born with blue eyes or brown, long noses or short, so also we are born with different emotional potentials, including a lesser or greater aggressive potential. What happens to this potential will partly depend on the external influences after the individual is born and comes into contact with the outside world. What do we see when we observe a newborn infant? Not much expression of love, but expression of need for warmth, food, comfort, cuddling, mothering. If the infant is cold, hungry, wet, uncomfortable, he expresses aggression by crying, or by screaming and other signs of rage.

Right here, we can see something which has far-reaching consequences for the destiny of the individual, of communities and nations. You can quiet the screaming, raging infant by relieving his discomfort, by keeping him warm and dry, satisfying his hunger. What is more important to understand is that cuddling and mothering alone will quiet the child for a time, even if he is not fed or changed. The opposite is also true, with consequences just as serious. Regardless of how comfortable we make the child, giving him all the food he wants, satisfying all his material needs, it will not be enough, will not eliminate anger unless he also receives mothering, cuddling, human warmth.

Later on, what do we observe in the growing child? A continuous, relentless drive to satisfy his needs. If we were to judge him by the standards of an adult in our society we would consider him a violent, destructive, anti-social psychopath, remorselessly concerned only with his own desires, with no regard for the interests or even the life of anyone else. Left to themselves, for example, little children may and sometimes do seriously harm a younger brother or sister.

It is the task of the family, of society, to change this little savage into a well-functioning member of our civilization. Not an easy task. *What he becomes will depend on his inherent potentials, the inner conflicts of maturation and the influence of his environment.* The aggressive drive can be cultivated, modified and utilized for constructive purposes or it can be channeled into increased violence. It can be blocked, "beaten out"—interfered with in many different ways, resulting in destructive behavior toward others and toward the self.

People are taken aback at the statement that man takes pleasure in violence. But we do not have to look far to observe this for ourselves. Anyone watching a child tear a fly to pieces, pull the tail of a cat, make a frog jump, invent games

45

of torture, cannot question his enjoyment. What about the injuries they inflict on each other—or their pleasure in watching violence on television?

As for adults—what about their enjoyment of hunting and fishing? I refer, of course, to those who do it purely for pleasure—the fishermen who don't eat the fish and the hunters who leave their prey to the vultures, except what they take home to mount as trophies. What about the fascination with prizefights, wrestling, violent competitive sports? "Push his face in!"—"Knock his teeth out!"—"Murder him!" It is not just the "sadists" and "degenerates" in the audience who scream these epithets but the normally mild-mannered ladies and gentlemen come to partake vicariously of the brutality they pay to witness.

What about bullfights, cockfights, the gladiators and the premiums they set on new and unusual ways of killing? Can we forget the Christians being torn to pieces by hungry lions, to the ecstatic roar of thousands of onlookers, great and humble, young and old, men and women? Can we forget the fiendish tortures of the Inquisition, the witch-hunts, the lynchings in our own country, the ultimate brutalities of the Nazis?

No, unless we deliberately choose to be blind, it is impossible to ignore the many ways in which man finds pleasure in violence—from the great American sport of kidding to the frequently dangerous practical jokes; from the cruelties of the initiation rites of primitive societies and of the fraternities of our great universities to the tortures and killings in persecutions and wars.

From the time the first primitive man tore his adversary to pieces with his teeth and his bare hands, mankind's scourge, his urge to kill, his passion for destruction have not changed. Moral codes, ethical concepts, the teachings of religion, punitive law, revenge and retribution have not changed it.

What is more, we cultivate our pleasure in violence. We give our children toys of destruction. We fill the air with violence for entertainment, from early morning till late at night. Television stations vie with each other to find new, unusual ways to kill. Newspaper headlines scream the grisly details of rape, mayhem, murder. And when we are old enough, we learn to use real weapons, to perfect "the art of killing"—out of real or imagined necessity. We may entice young men to "Join the Navy and See the World"— or "Join the Army and Learn a Trade"—but the main goal of military training always has been and always will be to perfect "the art of killing." The side benefits of discipline, of learning to live with one another, of mastering a trade, could be achieved much more effectively in an environment in which the teaching of this "art" was not involved.

During the successive phases of the libido

47

development, aggression and violence are expressed in various ways. The first use to which an infant puts his mouth is to suck and to scream. When he grows a little older, he acquires teeth and begins to bite. Obviously, biting is not just a means of inflicting pain. It is a necessary function to sustain life. We have to bite and chew our food to make it digestible. So, from the beginning, the child can use his mouth constructively to suck, to chew food, and simultaneously to inflict pain. All nursing mothers experience the child's pleasure in biting as well as sucking.

What can we do about it? We must teach our children to use their mouths constructively— to use language to express their emotions rather than physical force. If we can teach a child that to communicate anger with words is preferable to biting and inflicting pain, we will make him freer as an adult to express his feelings verbally rather than having to act them out. Words can express violence too—"The pen is mightier than the sword"—but better to curse and swear, if need be, than to annihilate physically.

Aggression is at its peak during the anal phase. The child can express anger by soiling himself, and temper tantrums are most frequent during this phase. Anal activities and eliminating or withholding are very effective ways of expressing violence, of defying the parents—especially if they gratify the child by being properly aggravated. And in adult life, which of us is unaware of the extent to which words connoting elimination are used to express rage? Yet, in spite of all the anti-social, violent, destructive desires which are common to all human beings, children can be guided to use the energy of this destructive potential in constructive ways.

The worst thing that can happen to children, especially during the first years of life, is to be forced into inactivity. Then they cannot learn to use aggressive energy constructively. One of the dangers of our civilization is our enforced passivity. There seems to be less and less reason to use our bodies, our aggressive energy purposefully. Most things are done for us by machines. Many of the labor-saving devices in the home and in industry are useful but by diminishing the need for activity they interfere with the constructive use of the aggressive drive. Why walk to the drugstore if you can drive there? Yet we would be much healthier if we did walk—and it is especially necessary for children to be active. This is one of the dilemmas of our society—how to permit a child all the activity he requires and at the same time teach him not to use it destructively. Nevertheless, it can be done as we gain understanding of human psychology and human needs.

During the phallic phase, children come increasingly into contact with the rest of the world. This is the period during which people think that boys should be encouraged to be aggressive *outside* the home, but not *inside*. It is especially important at this point in the child's development to teach him to use his energy constructively. Instead, we actually do the reverse. We encourage their pleasure in violence. We let them play with guns. They grow up equating violence with masculinity. Instead, it must be the task of adults to make children realize that a gun is not a phallic symbol, not a symbol of masculinity but a weapon designed for one purpose only—to maim, to kill.

On the other hand, it takes aggressive energy to seek a sexual partner in adulthood— to court, to insist, to win someone we desire and love. Without using aggressive energy, we would not be able to perform the sexual act. No one can deny that having intercourse with a virgin is an aggressive act. But this is normal, necessary aggression. If, as adults, we are incapable of distinguishing between the two, it can lead to serious sexual difficulties. It can result in impotence; or sexual activities will be used not for sexual gratification but in order to hurt the sexual partner.

Incidentally, a young child has no understanding of the act of intercourse. He may overhear his parents having intercourse, which happens more frequently than adults believe. To him, it sounds as though they are fighting. Then later on, he finds out about mentruation, that women bleed from the genitals. Somehow, he associates

50

the two and comes to believe that intercourse represents violence—that Father, that the penis, is hurting Mother. Healthy sex education could correct this misconception.

On the basis of our present knowledge about the aggressive drive, we might therefore summarize as follows:

1. Aggression is a drive inherent in all human beings.

2. The aggressive drive has enormous destructive potential, and destructive activities in man are accompanied by pleasure.

3. Even in the most mature individual, and the most civilized society, the *potential* for violent action is ever present.

4. On the other hand, the aggressive drive has force, energy, power which are needed for actions of all kinds; we could not function without it.

5. The greater the maturity of the individual and the culture of the society in which he lives, the smaller should be the destructive use of aggression.

6. Meaningful work, physical activity, satisfactory human relations are essential for the constructive use of aggressive energy.

7. The tools created by our technological society interfere with these human needs and result in increased, destructive use of aggression.

## 9. Ambivalence

Love and hate are the two most powerful feelings of which human beings are capable. They are our faithful companions throughout life. Take any great literary work, from the classics to the moderns, and what will you read about? Love and murder, love and death. The emphasis shifts from one to the other, but the subject remains the same.

The word ambivalence was coined by the psychiatrist, Eugen Bleuler, to describe the existence of contrary forces in general. Today, it is popularly used not just to express love and hate, but doubt, hesitation, indecision, etc. Psychoanalysis, however, restricts the term to mean the love and hate existing simultaneously in every human being toward a given person.

It is difficult for most people to admit that they can hate as well as love. How much more difficult to accept the fact that they can and do love and hate the same person simultaneously, even though most of the time they are not conscious of these conflicting feelings. After all, we have been taught all our lives that we must *love* not hate our parents, brothers, sisters, neighbors, husbands, wives. But do we?

Examples from daily life demonstrate ambivalence better than theoretical explanations can. What mother has not experienced the pleasure and pain of having her child run to her, crying, "Mommy, I love you"—hugging and biting her at the same time. The black-and-blue marks are a reminder of his love and his simultaneous need to hurt. The two go hand in hand. Ever get a letter from a child whose feelings you have hurt? "Dear Mother," it begins, and ends with, "I hate you! Love. . . ."

Think for a moment about all the love, respect and attention we shower on mothers . . . the gifts and honors we bestow on Mother's Day. What happens to these same wonderful mothers when they become mothers-in-law? Immediately, they are hated or ridiculed, made the butts of cruel, destructive jokes. Why? The mothers have not changed, they are the same mothers they always were. But now we see them with the reverse side of our ambivalent feelings.

Where do these angry feelings spring from? They spring from the attempt to deal with ambivalence by splitting its two components, love and hate. We love our mothers and hate our mothers-in-law. We love our wives and hate their mothers, and so on. But ambivalence is not so easy to eliminate. A husband, for example, may go on telling his wife for years what a wonderful person she is—at the same time expressing severe criticism of her mother. How perfect their life together would be if only her impossible mother were not around to make trouble all the time. The wife, being naturally competitive with her mother, is usually not displeased to hear this until, in a sudden outburst of anger, the loving husband says: "And you're just like your mother!"

Ambivalence exists in the very first relationship—that between mother and child—and it is characteristic of every relationship throughout life. The younger the child, the stronger the ambivalence, the more easily it finds expression. It reaches its height during the anal phase of development, at the age of two or thereabouts, when the child is beginning his struggle for independence, for identity. It becomes strongly manifest again during adolescence, in the final phase of growing from childhood to adulthood.

As we mature, our ambivalent feelings become less outspoken, more difficult to recognize. However, even though they never disappear completely, they need not interfere with mature relationships. The more mature we become, the more possible it becomes for us to love someone and yet tolerate some expression of the hate and anger that exist in every relationship. It interferes only if anger makes us feel so guilty that we can never express it or, what is worse, never permit ourselves to become aware that it exists. If this happens, then sooner or later, and when we least expect it, our anger will burst forth.

The more adult we are, the more we should be able to love with a minimum of hate. On the other hand, we should also be able to hate without guilt. Hate, if combined with compassion and a sense of social responsibility, can be a powerful force motivating us to become involved in the problems of our world, to act, to try to change things which need changing. If we can never permit ourselves to experience dissatisfaction, resentment, anger, anxiety, we are doomed to just sit back and do nothing.

In certain emotional illnesses, the compulsion neuroses, for instance, the ambivalent conflict can become so intense that it seriously interferes with functioning. People like this are incapable of ever deciding what is right and what is wrong; are beset by constant doubt about everything they do. The moment they make up their minds to go in one direction, they immediately think of an opposite possibility, until activity may be completely paralyzed.

Freud compared this with a train having a powerful engine hooked up at either end, each pulling at full speed. Tremendous energy is expended but nothing happens; the train does not move. Yet there is the constant danger that one of the forces may become more powerful than the other and that catastrophe will result.

Ambivalence can be responsible for the inability of a human being to establish relationships with others. He may be capable of feeling and expressing love but if his ambivalence is strong enough, hatred will win out and the relationship will be destroyed. There are excellent examples of this situation in literature, in Shakespeare's masterful characterization of Hamlet, for example. Hamlet demonstrates the struggle of ambivalence perfectly. Much as he craved love, he ended up destroying not only those he hated but also those he loved and who loved him and, finally, himself along with them.

# 10.   The Id and the Development of the Ego

The Id is the oldest, most primitive agency of the psychic structure. It contains the instinctual drives, the potentials for sexual development, aggressive development, all the potentials a human being inherits and is born with. It might be described as an uncharted territory, a jungle full of conflicting needs, drives, fears, contradictions and symbols. It is timeless and ageless. It is the raw material out of which human functioning develops.

The concept of the Id—that we come into the world with certain needs, drives, potentials—contradicts the almost universal belief, existing both before and after the discoveries of Freud, that human beings are born "blank," and that what they eventually become depends entirely on conditions and experiences after birth. Psychoanalysis does not minimize the importance of external and social influences, but maintains that what we become depends on the potentials we are born with and the internal conflicts of maturation, as well as the effects of the external environment.

The instinctual drives, the forces contained in the Id, push relentlessly for expression, demand instant satisfaction. But society bars the way, so the Ego, or the Self as it is also called, develops as a result of the interaction between the vast areas of the Id and the external environment. A prerequisite for healthy Ego development is an environment in which the newborn infant and the growing child will meet with frustrations as well as satisfactions. Time was when children were expected to be seen and not heard (preferably, not seen either). Their rights were limited to obeying orders without question. After the turn of the century, the attitude changed—children were suddenly discovered, as it were, and the 20th Century became "the century of the child."

As so frequently happens with a new discovery, the pendulum swung far in the opposite direction: suddenly, children had all the rights, parents none. Gradually, we learned that neither extreme was satisfactory, that the best approach lies somewhere in between. The earlier attitude ignored the child's legitimate feelings, needs, desires, and placed the emphasis almost exclusively on socialization. The later one neglected positive educational and disciplinary measures and concentrated on satisfying the child's desires without restraint.

This period coincided with the early days of psychoanalysis when the emphasis was largely on instinctual drives, when less was known about the function of the Ego and when it was believed that one should never frustrate a child. This was widely adopted by parents and teachers alike because it relieved them of responsibility. For a time, it is easy to deal with children in this way—it is so much simpler to yield than to prohibit. But the more we learn about the Ego, the more we realize that reasonable frustrations, prohibitions, restrictions, are inevitable and essential for healthy growth. From the day we are born, we have to learn to wait, to postpone pleasure and the satisfaction of our needs, to tolerate tension and pain.

Teaching this to an infant does not mean we should ignore him. Step by step, we must encourage him to tolerate, to postpone without becoming panicky, without mistrusting the world. The love the infant experiences stems not only from being fed but from the warmth, affection and availability of the mother to care for him and make him comfortable.

One of the first needs of the newborn infant is to have physical contact with the mother. This is largely interfered with in our society. There are as yet few hospitals where an infant is permitted to remain with his mother from the minute he is born. It is considered unhygienic for the baby and tiring for the mother. The fact is that under normal conditions the separation is not in the interest of either mother or child. At best, it is in the interest of the "efficient" functioning of the hospital.

Unfortunately, also, many of the gadgets in use today interfere with contact between mother and baby. We use bottles and plastic trays and what not. Young mothers are told the trays are "hygienic," easy to carry, easy to care for—"keeps the infant cool in hot weather"—"keeps the baby's back straight." It is so easy in our culture to sell anything which is advertised as novel, made of plastic and "scientific."

However, even under the most favorable circumstances, the moment the infant is born he is separated from the body of his mother, he is alone. His physical needs are no longer satisfied automatically. He experiences hunger, cold, all kinds of new sensations. He discovers parts of his body—a finger, a toe, the skin, the hands—and slowly, his entire body. This is pleasurable and unique. He is getting and giving pleasure with his own body. It is a step toward independence, toward the recognition that he is not totally dependent on others, that he has his own resources to satisfy some of his needs.

Of course, in the process of maturation he has to learn to give this up, to modify it, to get satisfaction from other human beings. People who have difficulty establishing satisfactory relationships with others may regress and return for satisfaction to their own bodies. This is the original, seemingly less complicated way, where no "rejection" is possible and where one is master of the relationship.

Every new experience contributes to the development of the Ego. After a while, the child begins to recognize parts of other people and eventually, whole persons, not just a face, a hand, but a mother, a father. As he becomes aware of a being detached from himself, he begins to imitate this separate being. He learns to smile as his mother smiles, to frown as she does, to imitate her movements and gestures. He imitates the sounds he hears and later, he learns to speak, to use language to express his needs, feelings, thoughts.

The process of identification plays an important role in the development of the Ego. As it continues to develop, the child not only imitates but slowly learns to identify with the important figures around him. Some identify more with the mother; others with the father. All children identify to some extent with both parents. As growth continues, children identify not only with their parents but with brothers, sisters and, increasingly, with others inside and outside the family.

The parents, of course, remain the first and most important figures with whom children identify, and it is important to recognize that they identify not only with the conscious but with the unconscious needs and attitudes of their parents.

Unconsciously, parents may encourage children to act out impulses they may be unaware of in themselves. People are generally puzzled when a youngster from a respectable, law-abiding family becomes a delinquent. Good parents, good school, good church—how has it come about? It can happen if the youngster has identified with the unconscious, anti-social, rebellious desires of a parent or an important adult in his environment.

There's not much point in telling a child to be good, if every time he is naughty there is a secretive smile on the face of a parent. One may punish him, but the child senses just the same that the parent is pleased with his behavior. Children are not only sensitive to our actions, but to our feelings—even those we try to hide. A mother may praise to high heaven a dish she is feeding to a young child but if she herself is disgusted with it, the child will sense it. In general, children do not become what we want them to be, or what we tell them to be, but what we, their parents, their most important models, are.

As time passes, parents cease to be the only influence affecting their children. All sorts of events in the real world, over which parents have no control, affect them. We cannot keep our children from getting hurt physically and emotionally as they are growing up. Neither can children help hurting their parents. The first step a child takes is its first step away from the mother.

The important thing is how parents react to this. On their reaction depends whether the child will take this first step earlier or later, or perhaps never.

Parents have very little control also over the physical illnesses which their children may suffer, yet these too influence their emotional development. All sorts of difficulties, expected and unexpected, arise during the course of growing up. Fortunately, however, growing, maturing, is an automatic and natural process for all living organisms—and children, especially those who have had a reasonably good start and whose Ego development has been encouraged, have considerable resistance to painful experiences. It takes a long time before serious harm is done to them.

Giving birth, raising children, understanding their needs are natural processes for mothers also, and one type of personality is not necessarily better than another. How parents react to their children often depends on what kind of response they get from them. Some children can make parents miserable from the day they are born. They can make them feel anxious, guilty, ashamed. It is also inevitable that when a woman gives birth to a child, especially the first time, anxieties she herself experienced as a child are reactivated. It is surprising that we don't see the effects of this even more often than we do.

In order to avoid misunderstandings, I

might add that we don't have to frustrate children wilfully. The home creates enough opportunities naturally. Adults have needs of their own. They need privacy, have things to do outside the nursery, have to sleep, are not always available. These things teach a child that he must learn to wait for what he wants. If families just live naturally, children have to put up with plenty of postponements and frustrations from the moment they are born until they grow up and leave home to establish their own adult lives.

## 11.  Functions of the Ego—Ego Defenses

There are two principles under which human beings function—the Pleasure Principle and the Reality Principle. The infant functions under the Pleasure Principle exclusively. He has no judgment, no ability to tolerate tension, to recognize reality. He knows only that he wants—immediately and without interference or restriction—what will give him pleasure and does not want anything that causes pain.

Adults cannot live by this principle because society does not permit it. It is a primary function of the Ego to transform the Pleasure Principle of childhood into the Reality Principle of adult life, which must take into account everything the external world represents. In spite of the innumerable restrictions of society, it should be possible for a mature person to function primarily under the Reality Principle, to find satisfactory solutions for his life. If he does not find them, it is not because they are not available but because he is incapable of dealing with reality, because he judges or misjudges it in terms of his own fears, needs, unacceptable desires. Of course there are exceptions to this premise, such as intolerable social conditions, persecutions, severe restrictions of personal freedom, crippling physical illness—situations in which the individual has no freedom of choice.

There are two realities for every individual, the external reality and the internal one. The external reality should be the same for everyone, but it is not because it is influenced by the internal reality of each individual. A red traffic light means, "Stop. Do not cross." As an external reality it is the same command for everyone. As an internal reality, it is not. To one person the red light means that it is a reasonable order, a necessary protection for all. In this case, the external and internal reality coincide and there is no conflict. Another person may interpret it as directed against him personally, so he resents it and refuses to obey. This discrepancy between his internal reality and the objective reality can be so great as to result in injury to himself or others.

Functions of the Ego include *Perception* and *Judgment*. The child has to learn what the expression on his mother's face means, whether it represents anger or affection. He must learn to perceive all kinds of impressions and to judge their meaning. From the external world he learns to recognize color, form, motion; objects and how they can be used; whether they are a source of pleasure or pain.

66

Recognizing and experiencing are not enough. The external experiences have to be *Integrated* into his developing personality. We may compare this with learning to drive a car. At first, we have to be cognizant of the clutch, the wheels, the brakes, the gas pedal; we have to master every motion separately. After a while, everything is coordinated, we can drive automatically and pay attention to where we are going. When the Ego becomes capable of integrating external experiences into its psychic structure, it can pay attention to what we are doing. It can promote *Motility* and give direction to it.

If we are to learn from our experiences, we have to be able to remember them. *Memory* helps us to seek out what is desirable, reliable, pleasurable, and to avoid what is dangerous, painful. Memory is essential also to the acquisition of knowledge.

The use of *Language* is another Ego function. It requires a certain Ego maturity before a child can learn to speak. How well he will do will depend on his early experiences in communicating with the world—especially on the extent to which the mother is capable of communicating with and teaching the child. It will depend on whether the child is encouraged to use sounds or to be quiet. If, in order to keep him quiet, his needs are always anticipated even before he opens his mouth or, if he is punished too often for crying or being noisy, he will encounter difficulties in using language because he never learned the need for it or because he is afraid to use it.

If a mother were to ask me what is the most important thing to teach a child, I would say: "Teach him to use words, instead of just to act. Teach him to use properly one of the few tools human beings possess over the other animals —language with which to really communicate with others." An ability to use language teaches us the similarities as well as the many differences in the world. If we are to have satisfactory relations with others, we have to learn that people are different from one another; we have to learn not to fear these differences but to tolerate, accept, even appreciate them. If we all felt and thought alike, there would be no challenge in human relationships.

A multitude of functions—Learning, Judging, Integrating, Remembering, Reality Testing—contribute to the Ego's ability to adapt to the external world. To adapt means to accept the necessary restrictions of society which regulate human behavior and relationships. Adaptation is a process which continues as long as we live, because we must constantly meet changing conditions. If we have an Ego which is incapable of adjusting to change, then we cling rigidly to attitudes, ideas, fears which have long since lost their validity, and we permit them to govern our lives even though they are totally unrealistic.

One of the great difficulties we face in our modern world is the need to adjust constantly to rapidly changing situations. The more primitive the society, the more predictable is the life it affords, generation after generation. Very little adaptation is required. When we consider all the changes we have had to adjust to in the past twenty-five years alone, it is not surprising that there is such an increase in anxiety in the world today.

Another important function of the Ego is to help us establish satisfactory relations with other people. Without these there is no possibility of deriving instinctual satisfactions. The ability to relate to others will be strongly influenced by the experiences of infancy, as we have seen.

A well-developed Ego not only has the task of mediating between the instinctual drives and the external world but must find ways also to satisfy the demands of the Superego, or Conscience which, in our civilization, is primarily a prohibiting one. It must create the conditions under which harmonious functioning with the Superego is possible.

It must also provide energy for defenses. The purpose of all defenses, whether they are successful or not, is to avoid the painful emotions of severe anxiety, guilt and shame. I am not referring to a normal degree of these feelings, which are appropriate in certain given situations, but to their pathological manifestations which interfere with functioning. Yet we are brought up to accept the mores and prohibitions of our society almost exclusively by inculcating in us a sense of guilt, of shame.

One of the more successful Ego defenses is *Sublimation*—expressing one's own needs in a manner so socially acceptable that they elicit praise and recognition instead of disapproval or punishment. Sublimation may find expression in all manner of artistic creations, in writing, singing, lecturing, teaching, etc. All of these stem from our original libidinal and aggressive drives which were not permitted direct expression and had to be transformed, sublimated, in the process of growing up.

Many operas furnish good examples of violence combined with its sublimation in beautiful music. The stories they tell are all about torture, murder, death, accompanied by the most stirring vocal and orchestral music. They offer the listener the height of esthetic pleasure while at the same time enabling him to witness the death of a hero or a beautiful young maiden, or the incantation of a fearful curse.

Sublimation, however, is not the only successful Ego defense. It is healthy functioning if the Ego is capable of utilizing any defense which is suitable for a given situation; if it does not rigidly react to every situation with the same defense which has proven unsuccessful over and over again in the past.

Another Ego defense, similar in its external manifestations to sublimation, is *Reaction Formation*. This means doing exactly the opposite of the original forbidden desire. Sublimation and Reaction Formation are sometimes difficult to differentiate. One's choice of a profession may be motivated by either one of these defenses. We choose a certain profession because it affords a healthy outlet for some unconscious need. We know that children can be cruel, take pleasure in inflicting pain on others and torturing animals, both in reality and in their fantasies. Becoming a doctor or a surgeon permits sublimation of these impulses. A surgeon has to cut into people, but he does it to relieve pain, to cure. Sublimation should eliminate anxiety, yet there are few surgeons who can work without anxiety, because surgery comes too close to the original impulses. Therefore, the choice of this profession can represent either sublimation or reaction formation.

Reaction Formation explains the violence with which some anti-vivisectionists oppose the use of animals for research. Many of them have never witnessed any of this research but they have wild and destructive fantasies about what it must be like. If you tell them that for most experiments the animals are put to sleep, they refuse to believe it. There is some reality behind their fantasies, because human beings are cruel to animals and to each other, and because there is considerable unnecessary animal experimentation, not just for medical purposes. However, it is not only the reality but their fantasies which are behind most of the violent objections. The experimenter and the objector may have the same repressed fantasies of violence, they just deal with them differently.

*Denial* and *Projection* are very primitive Ego defenses, because they originate in earliest childhood, and they are frequently encountered. Denial helps us to avoid recognizing the existence within us of something which would evoke anxiety, guilt or shame. Projection makes us see it instead in someone else, like seeing ourselves in a mirror and believing that the image in the mirror is someone else. Of course the process is unconscious, but it is easy to demonstrate if we watch how children behave when they are afraid of punishment. A child is reprimanded for something he has done. For fear he will be punished, he insists that he didn't do it, even though he knows perfectly well that he did. The next step is automatic. He not only denies that he did it, but insists that his brother did it, or his sister did it, or the cat did it, anybody but he himself.

A universal Ego defense is *Repression.* Repression means that we keep out, or push out of consciousness something painful, or unacceptable, or dangerous, and deal with it as if it never existed. The existence of repression is one of the cardinal concepts of psychoanalytic theory and psychoanalytic therapy. Repression and the concept of the Unconscious are so intimately interrelated that they are inseparable. Anyone who rejects the defense of repression rejects the concept of the Unconscious and, therefore, psychoanalysis.

*Isolation,* separating things from each other which belong together, is another Ego defense. It means pigeonholing ideas and trying to deal with each conflict separately. We can isolate actions from feelings. We can isolate love from hate, the two components of ambivalence. Some people isolate feelings from thoughts. They can have destructive fantasies but have no feeling of guilt about them. Sometimes, when something terribly painful happens to a loved one, or to ourselves, it may even be healthy to deny the existence of the problem altogether so that we may go on functioning. However, when it is all over, we may go to pieces. When the person we love no longer needs our help, we can afford to break down. This is why so many soldiers who function well in combat break down after they are out of danger.

There is one Ego defense that is highly valued in our culture. We call it *Intellectualization*. Instead of feeling, such people talk and act primarily on the basis of intellect alone. Yet even though our society puts a premium on it, human beings cannot function successfully on the basis of intellect alone. If they do, they are like machines, human computers, who can give you all the facts about atomic war but have no feelings about it. They are just giving you figures when they tell you how many millions of human beings will be destroyed in the first few minutes, the first hour, the first day of an atomic attack. For them these millions are just mathematical calculations, not living people. Human computers are people who intellectualize in order to eliminate feelings, and to separate them from thinking about their actions. That is why they are a menace to the world we live in.

Each one of the Ego defenses can be a healthy defense in a given situation; or it can be a pathological one which interferes with our functioning. If we rigidly adhere to one set of defenses —if, for example, we use denial and projection so that we can never recognize violence in ourselves but only in others, then we are in trouble.

When the discrepancy between the instinctual needs and the prohibitions against them is so great that most of the energy available to the Ego must be used to maintain rigid defenses, then there is little energy left for functioning. What we are doing then is to use the available energy we need for living, working, satisfying our desires, to protect ourselves from the painful feelings of anxiety, guilt and shame.

## 12. The Superego (The Conscience)

We know that the child identifies with his parents and, subsequently, with other important figures in the world about him. He not only identifies with their needs and actions, but also with their attitudes. Identifying with these attitudes marks the beginning of the development of the Superego, or the Conscience. As he grows up, the moral codes of his parents and the racial and family traditions they represent; the moral concepts and ideals of the civilization of which he is a part, are incorporated into his Superego, his Conscience.

Freud called the Superego the heir to the Oedipus complex. When the boy, afraid of his powerful father, stops competing with him, he identifies with him, with his prohibitions and controls and makes them his own. It is not until the fifth or sixth year of life that the Conscience thus becomes established in the inner makeup of a human being. The forerunners of the Conscience date back to the first time the child experiences restrictions and prohibitions from the external world. We see small children say "no" to themselves and spank their own hands when they do something they have been taught not to do. But this is still just imitation. Only when these attitudes become the child's own inner attitudes and prohibitions can we speak of his having a Conscience.

The objection is often raised that psychoanalysis ignores the external environment and concerns itself only with intra-psychic conflicts. If we comprehend how the Ego and the Superego develop, it is not difficult to see how this misconception arises. The Ego (the Self) and the Superego (the Conscience) evolve as a result of the interaction between the drives and potentials of the Id and the external world. When, as the individual matures, they become part of his psychic structure, then the conflicts he experiences between his desires and his prohibitions become internalized, even though they originated in conflicts with the external world.

Not that we find this easy to accept. We try to delude ourselves that the conflicts result from external forces because it is easier to deal with them than with our inner prohibitions and conflicts. "The right hand doesn't know what the left hand does," is an evasive attempt to avoid responsibility and therefore punishment by one's own conscience. However, the right hand does know what the left hand does. We can hide from outside authorities, but we cannot forever hide from ourselves. Sooner or later, every child learns that parents are not omniscient. If we don't tell them something, they won't know about it. If we lie, they won't know we are lying. This discovery comes both as a relief and a tremendous disappointment. It is the beginning of the individual's functioning within the privacy of his own thinking, feeling and acting.

In the early teens, this leads to the familiar dialogue: "Where have you been?"—"Out."—"What did you do?"—"Nothing." This simply means that the child is holding out for his own freedom and privacy. Of course this entails individual responsibility. People who can accept responsibility for their actions have well-functioning Superegos and are capable of acting independently without constantly worrying about what others may think or say.

Let us consider again the misconception that psychoanalysis ignores social conditions and the external environment. When we assert that Conscience develops through accepting and identifying with the moral and social codes of the environment, it should be obvious that what is acceptable in one society is not necessarily so in another. Nor is it the same for everyone within the framework of any given society. The code of a gang is different from that of society at large. The conscience of a religious man operates differently from that of an atheist.

In a poverty-stricken slum it is taken for granted that it is better to steal food than to go hungry. A member of such a community would regard this as normal. His conscience would not trouble him, he would not feel guilty. In a more prosperous milieu, a 14-year-old who steals is regarded as sick or delinquent. However, he may be neither. His action may simply reflect the internal concept of right and wrong he has gained from his environment. Or it may result because he never experienced reasonable discipline in the home.

On the other hand, a youngster from an underprivileged, persecuted environment, who learns the hard way that restrictions and prohibitions exist only to punish him, will not accept the laws of society, he will rebel against them. For him, this is normal behavior. It cannot and should not be treated as sickness. That it is anti-social is not his fault, it is the fault of the society which let him grow up in a milieu where this was the only way to develop a personality, an Ego, a Superego.

Generally, when people refer to the Superego, they speak of it in terms of interfering with our actions, prohibiting, making us feel guilty. Actually, the function of a healthy Superego is not only to restrict and punish, but to make us feel worthy, satisfied with ourselves, to enhance our feeling of well-being.

There are many forms of Conscience, depending on the influences we have absorbed from the authority figures during childhood. For example, there is usually a considerable discrepancy between what we think we ought to be, what we think people expect us to be, and what we really are. The more impossible the ideal we set for ourselves, the less likelihood there is of achieving it and the more difficult it becomes to appease our Conscience. We may end up by never being satisfied with anything we do.

If one can be satisfied only if he plays the violin as well as Heifetz, or writes as well as Shakespeare, anything below this standard will seem worthless, not worth attempting. If we take literally such slogans as, "All men are created equal" —or, "Any American can become President"— then of course we can only blame ourselves if we do not achieve the highest levels. By the same token, parents who may have spent thousands of dollars for violin lessons for their child may feel that if he doesn't play as well as Heifetz it can only be because he is lazy and never practices enough. This is absurd, of course, because it ignores individual differences and innate talent or the lack of it.

Then there is the type of Conscience that makes us feel guilty or anxious about anything we do that is pleasurable. It makes a difference in the development of the Conscience whether, in

early childhood, the prohibitions which were enforced were primarily against expressions of aggression, against sexual activity, or against both.
Rarely are the prohibitions against both equal.
Some children grow up in an atmosphere where
aggression is encouraged and all sexuality severely
prohibited. Others are forbidden any expressions
of anger or violence in the home but not outside
it. The result is utter confusion and suffering.

The worst victims are the thousands
upon thousands of emotional cripples among combat soldiers in the wake of every war. It was called
"shell shock" in the First World War and "combat
neurosis" in the Second World War. However,
whatever it is called, the shock has nothing to do
with the shells but with the irreconcilable conflicts engendered between violence, torture, killing
on the one hand and the Conscience which forbids
them on the other. Untold numbers of men, com-
manded all their lives, "Thou shalt not kill" who,
as soldiers are not only ordered to kill but are
severely punished if they cannot or will not, and
are celebrated as heroes if they perform well,
crack up under the conflicts thus engendered within themselves.

The Conscience can be harsh, cruel,
making us suffer, pay a price for every achievement, for every pleasure. "Don't ever say business
is good"—"Don't boast about your success or you'll
pay for it"—"Don't be too pretty or the Evil Eye

will get you"—these are expressions of a Conscience which prohibits pleasure or success, which demands that we pay for pleasure with pain.

There are many people in our culture who believe that pain and pleasure are inevitably interlocked. There are those who can never enjoy the sunshine because they are too busy saving for a rainy day; those who crave the cake but have to postpone eating it until they no longer have any appetite for it. These are all restrictions that an individual's own guilty Conscience inflicts on him because of attitudes incorporated from the external world.

There are other forms of the Superego, like the "Forgiving Conscience": "I'll think about it tomorrow."—"Let's not worry about it now, let's do it first." There is what I like to call the "Retroactive Conscience," or the "I wish I hadn't done it" Conscience which, however, rarely stops an individual from doing what he later wishes he hadn't done. These are the acting-out or impulse-ridden characters who want something, act upon it immediately and worry about it later, often paying by being severely punished for what they have done.

There are also people who constantly expose themselves to punishment by committing anti-social acts under conditions which assure that they will be caught. In extreme cases, there are those who confess to crimes they have never committed because they feel as guilty as if they had committed them. This, too, springs from our culture which has taught for centuries that an evil thought is as bad as an evil deed. Well, we can't control our thoughts and feelings, yet even the most destructive emotions and desires are harmless if we don't act on them. The more we deny their existence, the greater the danger that we will act on them when we least expect it.

We try to bribe our Consciences in many ways. We bargain with ourselves: "If I mow the lawn or clean the garage, I can then play golf."— "If I skip desserts for a week, I can buy a new blouse." We bribe our Consciences just as we tried to bribe our parents when we were children, by promising to do this if they would let us have that. By the time we reach adulthood, the conflicts have become internalized and we are bargaining with ourselves, not with the outer world. All those good New Year resolutions are attempts to live up to the demands of the Conscience.

The Superego represents the laws of our inner world and, as pointed out earlier, there are no laws in either the inner or outer world against those things people don't want to do in the first place. In some individuals, the internal restrictions are stronger than the external ones but for the majority of human beings external laws are an absolute necessity. Freud has said that if we were to eliminate all laws and punishments in our society, there would undoubtedly be a great increase in all crimes except patricide and incest. Prohibitions against patricide and incest do not originate in the environment after we are born. We bring them with us; they belong to our phylogenetic development. The history of the human race is expressed in them.

There are certain chemical substances which interfere not only with the functioning of the Ego but even more with the Superego. We might say, for example, that the Conscience is soluble in alcohol. It can also be diluted by gang formation. Gangs of youngsters or mobs of adults can commit acts together which none of them could commit individually. Afterwards they cannot understand how they came to participate in anything so violent and destructive without any guilt feelings, with even a feeling of pleasure.

Many people do things under the influence of alcohol which they would not do otherwise. This need not necessarily be pathological. Alcohol can have a relaxing effect on a strong and forbidding Conscience which does not permit one to do even things one should not be afraid to do. This lessening of tension can sometimes be desirable, but excessive drinking is another matter. Some who become violent may otherwise be quite mild and gentle. The point is, why are they usually so mild? It is because they cannot permit themselves even normal expressions of anger until they are under the influence of alcohol, or until they are asleep and we learn that most of their dreams are filled with violence and destruction. The difference, however, between violence expressed in dreams and violence under the influence of alcohol is that in sleep, we are immobilized, we cannot act. If sufficiently intoxicated, we can and do.

We make a big issue of smoking. Why not of drinking? Perhaps a smoker can smoke himself to death, but he doesn't hurt anyone except himself. On the other hand, an alcoholic not only hurts himself but is also a menace to others. Statistics prove that much violence—killing in the home, on the street, on the highways—and many other major crimes are committed under the influence of alcohol. Still, no serious attempts have been made to educate people to the dangers of drinking. On the contrary, aping their elders and responding to the seduction of advertising, teenagers consider it sophisticated adult behavior, a requirement for social acceptance.

It is even more amazing to think of all the existing laws against the sale, the use, even the possession of a large variety of drugs, but there are practically none against the sale, the possession and the use of firearms.

The pressures exerted upon us by the Superego create feelings of guilt. Guilt is one of the most painful, devastating emotions which befall us. Our culture is governed by it. We are raised with it, struggle with it all our lives, suffer, try to get rid of it by denying it, blaming others, making others feel guilty in the hope that if we succeed, we can get rid of our own guilt.

Regardless of where we search for the source of guilt feelings—whether we study religions, history, the relations between nations, the family, or the analysis of an individual, we inevitably arrive at the conflicts arising from human violence: the command—"Thou shalt not kill"— and the inability of human beings to heed the prohibition; the need to go on hurting and killing. All sorts of rationalizations are employed to justify this evil necessity of mankind, in order to suppress guilt. "Thou shalt not kill" is inevitably followed by the footnote, "Unless . . ."—listing innumerable conditions under which killing is not only permissible but highly desirable, even a virtue. The price we pay is physical and emotional suffering; ever-increasing violence to justify violence; and often enough, self-destruction.

It is difficult enough to deal with conscious guilt; even more so with unconscious guilt. Guilt is the motivating force of suicide. It explains why the suicide rate is highest in affluent societies, lowest among those who are persecuted and punished, like the Negroes in our country. If we are punished by external forces, we do not have to feel guilty and punish ourselves.

What makes children spank their own hands, provoke punishment from adults? Guilt. What makes the criminal return to the scene of his crime? Guilt. What makes people confess to crimes they never committed? Guilt. What makes people provoke all kinds of self-punishment—cutting a finger every time they pick up a knife; having one accident after another whether in the home or outside? Guilt. Why do people beat their breasts in a church or synagogue? What is the meaning of *"Mea Culpa"*? Guilt. What makes people go to Confession? Guilt. What causes the depression of those who have survived persecutions, concentration camps, combat? The major cause of all depressions and its most torturing symptom is Guilt.

Quite commonly people emerge from a depression if they suffer physical injury, as if their physical suffering substitutes for their emotional suffering. They do not have to feel guilty while suffering bodily pain. Usually, they become depressed again as soon as the physical pain disappears. There have been famous men in history who could only use their talents and become successful after suffering severe physical illness or injury; when they no longer experienced guilt about unconscious needs and fantasies. The opposite is also true. Many great talents have never come to fruition because of overwhelming guilt feelings.

Even though there are differences between group psychology and the psychology of the individual, there are enough similarities so that we may be justified in drawing certain parallels. Guilt feelings resulting from violent desires or actions can be observed in both the behavior of individuals and nations. Attempts to justify violence in the hope of getting rid of guilt are very similar in both, are equally unsuccessful and, in the end, equally self-destructive. The alternative, the road to healthy functioning, lies in the recognition of the source of guilt in our own violent natures.

## 13. Fixation and Regression

Normally, a living organism, whether plant, animal or human, presses steadily toward growth and it takes a great amount of opposing pressure to interfere seriously with this normal process of maturation. This does not mean that growing is a continuous, forward-moving process. Even healthy development encompasses moving ahead, stopping sometimes, even going backwards sometimes.

*Fixation* means remaining fixed, arrested at some phase of development so that there is no further progress. *Regression* means that in spite of having progressed to a higher level of functioning, we revert to an earlier behavior pattern.

How does fixation come about? Why should a child remain fixed primarily on pleasures related to the mouth when he should have developed further? There are two important causes—over-indulgence or severe frustration during the oral phase of development. Worse than either, is to alternate between the two. If from the earliest days something is put into the child's mouth every time he opens it, it will be difficult to give up oral pleasure and will discourage any incentive to act on his own. Severe frustration has the same effect as over-indulgence. The emphasis here is on *severe* frustration. Reasonable frustrations are necessary from the beginning, to help the child learn that he is not completely helpless, that he can do some things for himself.

This is when we must start to teach children to tolerate tension, to postpone satisfaction. People who cannot learn this can never experience complete satisfaction. Just imagine that you always have before you a table filled with good things to eat, and every few minutes you walk up to it and nibble something. Pleasurable, yes, but you will never know what it means to satisfy hunger because you will never have experienced hunger. So, in the long run, over-indulgence results in loss of pleasure.

In regression, a child reverts to behaving as he did months, or even years, earlier. Physical illness may cause it. It may occur under the pressure of weaning or toilet training. It occurs almost automatically during a mother's subsequent pregnancy, even if a child pretends not to notice the mother's condition.

This is especially true for the first-born. Even though every child wants to be the only child, the first-born alone experiences this particular situation. He reacts with the greatest disturbance to the birth of another baby, considers it a betrayal on his mother's part. For some time, he has been the only one. Now he must watch his mother nurse, feed, clean a new baby. He wants everything the infant gets. Even though he may have given up the bottle long ago, he now wants it again. He may have been dry for quite a while, but he begins to wet again. He is saying: "I'm just as helpless as the other one. I have to be taken care of just like the new baby." This is also an effective way of expressing his anger. Soiling, wetting are messy, aggravating, keep Mother busy and draw her attention away from the new infant.

Parents are sometimes frightened when this happens, or they may ridicule or punish the child. Of course it is a problem, but it is not an illness. If it is handled with tolerance and reasonable discipline, difficulties may not ensue and it may mark another step on the road to maturation. When the mother is busy with the new-born baby, the older children may learn increasingly to rely on themselves.

## 14. Normality

Psychoanalysis, being a comprehensive theory of human psychology, is as deeply engaged in investigating what constitutes normal behavior as abnormal behavior. The more we delve into the subject, however, the more we realize that normalcy is not easy to define; its variations cover a broad field. What is normal for one person is not necessarily so for another. What constitutes normal behavior in one culture is far from normal in another. Much confusion and misunderstanding arise from the tendency of nations as well as individuals to establish their own norms and to apply them to everybody else.

It is of the utmost importance to realize that there is a wide range within which we would have to consider a person normal who, under certain stresses, may temporarily show symptoms or a pattern of behavior which in someone else, under other circumstances, would be considered pathological. This is comparable to the range within which we consider various conditions or functions of the body normal. We talk about the range of normal for blood sugar, cholesterol, every other chemical component of the blood. Or the average range for weight, blood pressure, pulse, respiration, etc., yet even these averages change at different ages, under stress, even at different times of the day. When we are rested, peaceful, blood pressure and pulse go down; when we are angry or anxious, they go up, yet both may be within the range of normal.

Nevertheless, we must try to arrive at some understanding of what we mean by normal. What criteria does an analyst use to determine whether an individual is normal or not? He cannot judge normality from the content of the individual's Unconscious or Id, because in the Unconscious of every human being there exist fiercely conflicting instinctual drives, murderous impulses, death wishes against those we love, although in real life we are not criminals at all but quite possibly doctors, lawyers, judges, artists, ministers. He cannot judge normality by what an individual dreams because the distortions in dreams are more or less common to all of us; and the attempted solutions for our conflicts in dreams are substantially the same for all of us.

Well, if the analyst cannot judge normalcy from the content of the Unconscious or of dreams, perhaps he should be able to rely on the manifestations of the Superego. But can he? Most people take it for granted that anyone with a strong Superego, with strict moral standards, is healthy, normal. But he is not necessarily so. Psychotics may have the highest moral standards, yet they are very sick. A criminal may have a very strict, punishing Conscience, so strict that he may even commit a crime out of his sense of guilt, in order to provoke punishment. So it is clear that the Superego alone does not tell us either whether someone is sick or healthy.

Where does the analyst go from here? To the Ego of the individual. It is the Ego which is responsible for finding acceptable outlets for our instinctual needs, mediating between those needs, external reality, and the internal prohibitions of our own Conscience. Theoretically, the prerequisite for normality would be the harmonious functioning together of all three psychic forces, the Id, the Ego and the Superego within the individual— and to achieve this desirable end would of course require a perfectly functioning Ego.

A perfectly functioning Ego would be able to integrate our internal needs and our external experiences. It would be able to control and direct our libidinal and aggressive needs and energies into satisfying and worthwhile channels. It would have a faultless memory, recalling everything without distortion, since this is the best way we can learn to utilize experience. It would not only make motility possible but would be able to control our actions and to recognize and avoid dangerous situations. It would be able to use intellect: thought and actions would not be under the influence of the emotions alone. It would use language primarily for purposes of communication, not to hurt or punish.

Ideally, then, normalcy would include the ability to always judge reality objectively— never to project our own hostile impulses and perceive them as dangers from outside ourselves. It would include the ability to know who we are, what we are, what our needs and desires are, and to accept them even if we do not like them. Normalcy would mean not only being able to accept responsibility for our actions, but for our fantasies and dreams as well, which would require anxiety-free and guilt-free communication with the Unconscious.

Of course, on this perfect plane, we would have to admit that no such animal as a normal person exists. No Ego, no individual, functions this perfectly physically or emotionally. There are too many internal and external determinants which make it impossible. Even if it were possible, it would not be desirable. Life would be predictable, monotonous, without challenge.

In a word, the range of normalcy is very broad. It is normal to be depressed and to mourn the loss of a loved one at the time of loss and for a period following it; not so normal if the depression continues indefinitely or if we only begin to feel depressed years after the event. It is normal

to suffer anxiety when we are faced with a dan
gerous situation, like having to cross a boulevard
against the lights; not so normal if we cannot leave
the house at all for fear we may have to cross a
boulevard. Failure and pain are as much a part
of normal living as success and pleasure. We all
use poor judgment sometimes, make mistakes,
have serious problems—but this does not mean we
are sick. A psychoanalyst must very carefully assess
an individual's problems and symptoms before he
can decide whether he is dealing with a sick person or one who is struggling with unavoidable and
realistic difficulties.

However, there are some realistic criteria
by which we may define a normal person. He is
an individual who is capable of satisfactory relations with others; who can love someone other
than himself; who is capable of working, playing,
accepting responsibilities, tolerating pain, enjoying himself. Such a person does not react to every
success with, "Look how great I am!" . . . to every
failure with, "Everything happens to me."

My favorite description of a normally
functioning human being is one who, in spite of
all the necessary restrictions of society and the
complexities of existence can find a satisfactory
solution for his life. What is satisfactory for one
person is not necessarily so for another; nor does
satisfaction mean continuous happiness. People
talk longingly of achieving happiness as a goal in

life, but this is not realistic. No one can be happy all the time. Living entails much pain, many difficulties under the best of circumstances, and at least some pleasures even under the worst of circumstances.

When we recall our childhood, we have a tendency to remember only what suits our needs. To refer to them as "the good old days" is just as distorted as, "I had a perfectly miserable childhood." During analysis, "Nobody ever gave me anything" is revealed as an expression of a patient's anger against his world of today, as well as the world of his childhood. As his analysis proceeds and he finds it possible to give up more and more of his anger, he begins to recall some very pleasurable experiences during his "miserable childhood." Father wasn't always a "bastard" and Mother didn't really neglect him "by going out every night." As a matter of fact, she often didn't leave the house for weeks on end. After a while the patient recalls that, "Well, yes, Father did give me a bicycle"—and then adds quickly, "But not when I asked for it, and it wasn't the model I wanted." He also begins to remember that when he was given something, it made him angrier than when he was refused. It's a dirty trick when parents who had to be proven to be ogres turn out not to be; it interferes with one's need to blame them for everything.

People who have to blame everyone but

themselves for their problems become depressed every time something good happens to them because then they cannot justify their anger, they can only feel guilty about it. They have to fight against all pleasures, have to feel miserable, neglected, rejected. As a patient once remarked: "The better I get, the worse I feel." The feeling of well-being is prohibited to them as all pleasures are prohibited, unless they pay a high price for them.

So long as we have to prove that all our misery is caused by forces outside ourselves, we have to fight feeling well, functioning well. We have to try to defeat what analysis strives to achieve. If an analysis is successful, we must eventually give up blaming the world and recognize that our misery is of our own making, that even if in the past there was justification for blaming others, that justification has long since lost its validity. Even though we were helpless as children, we are not helpless as adults, we can make our own way in the world.

When, for various reasons, the Ego cannot maintain the balance required for healthy functioning, conflicts arise and emotional disturbances may follow. We must always bear in mind that we are all born with varying intensities of needs and with greater or lesser ability to adjust to the requirements of the external world and to tolerate tension. Obviously, the greater the pressure of our drives, the more difficult it is to adjust to prohibitions, to give up some desires altogether, modify others, postpone still others in order to achieve eventual satisfaction.

Furthermore, under certain conditions even a well-functioning adult may become emotionally disturbed. There is no Ego which does not have a limit of tolerance, a breaking point beyond which it cannot put up with tension. Some people can tolerate a great deal; others very little. People who have generally had an easy time of it find it terribly difficult to tolerate frustrations. An illness or injury, the loss of a loved one, any number of events beyond our control may mobilize unconscious, internal conflicts and lead to disturbances of the balance between the psychic agencies. The character and intensity of the disturbances will depend on the Ego of the individual.

The more energy the Ego has to expend to build up defenses, in order to keep unacceptable desires under control, the less will be available for all its other functions. It is like having an army in reserve, or money in a savings account which we can use if we need to. If we have very little Ego energy in reserve, then of course the breakdown and the conflict preceding the breakdown will occur much faster. Even if we have a great deal in reserve, it may not be enough because everyone has a limit of tolerance. When we reach this limit, some or all of the Ego functions, such as reality testing, judgment, perception, sublimation, motility, ability to work, are impaired or cease to operate altogether. Now the Ego must use all its energy to maintain defenses against intolerable feelings of guilt, shame, anxiety.

First, let us look at those occurrences to which anyone will react with temporary disturbance, such as physical illness, an injury, a tragedy. The first reaction to illness is that we regress. This is normal and goes hand in hand with the need to be taken care of. If we can passively accept the necessary care, as we did when we were children, we have a good chance to recover. If we fight against it, our chances are diminished. We have all seen both types of patients in any hospital: those who gladly accept the only benefit to be derived from illness and pain, being taken care of, and those who have to fight constantly to deny that they are helpless. People do senseless things to prove that they do not need help, especially when they need it most.

When we lose someone we love, we react with mourning and depression. This, too, is normal. The intensity of the reaction again depends on the kind of Ego we have. When we are ill, we need someone to look after us. When we suffer bereavement, we usually want to be left alone. It is in the nature of man to endure pain alone and to want to share pleasure with others. Mourning can result in serious emotional disturbances which may have all the symptoms of severe illness. Yet it is not an illness unless it lasts beyond reason. It requires understanding, judgment on the part of those near to us to know when not to intrude.

We are living in a time when the word "anxiety" has become anathema. Billions of pills are sold and swallowed for the purpose of ridding us of anxiety. Why? Normal anxiety is essential for self-preservation. It warns us of possible dangers. If we succeed in ridding ourselves of it too quickly, we do not perceive the dangers that may be threatening us from outside or within ourselves. Anxiety prompts us to take action—either to face the danger or to take steps to avoid it. If we respond appropriately, the anxiety will have served its purpose and will disappear.

In the face of danger, there are three possible ways to react: flight, fight, or paralysis. It is up to the Ego to judge whether standing up and fighting—or running away—is the reasonable thing to do. If the anxiety becomes too great, it will interfere with the Ego's ability to make a sensible judgment. When this occurs, we become paralyzed or act irrationally.

There is, however, a pathological form of anxiety based on repressed, unconscious drives and conflicts which is all-pervasive and terribly destructive. One day it makes us afraid to cross a street; the next day we are terrified of making any decisions; the third day we do not dare tell someone he is doing something wrong; or we become petrified of our employer; or we don't dare to discharge an incompetent employee. We blame the particular situation disturbing us for our anxiety, when it has nothing to do with it. The fact is that because of this "free-floating anxiety" we are incapable of judging what is or is not really dangerous to us. It helps not at all to blame external forces for our inability to reason, to act, because this anxiety is connected with conflicts carried over from childhood which have long since lost their meaning but have lived on in our Unconscious.

There are people who suffer less from anxiety but instead, from a permanent sense of guilt. That they have done nothing to warrant this makes no difference at all: they just feel guilty, accused, in constant danger of punishment. Anxiety, guilt and shame do not exist in a vacuum. We experience them in relation to other people or to external situations. So it may seem reasonable, when such feelings overwhelm us, to withdraw into ourselves, to avoid contact with others. What happens if we do? We become lonely, complain bitterly that no one cares for us. It is a justifiable complaint even if it is of our own making. If we avoid every situation which may provoke anxiety or guilt; if we do not permit anyone to come near us, we may succeed in overcoming anxiety or guilt but we are left alone, depressed, filled with self-hatred.

The nature of the particular emotional illness to which we may succumb will depend on our psychic structure, our inborn potentials, the experiences of our childhood, our cultural milieu, and the vicissitudes of life. The disturbance may be purely emotional, or may find expression in physical symptoms, or in a combination of the two. To go into detail about the great variety of emotional disturbances which characterizes our civilization is beyond the scope of this book.

## 15. Obstacles to Growth: Automobiles and Television

Physical activity, play, experiencing one's own ability to discover things, to master things, to do new things alone and with others, are essential for healthy growth. Anything that interferes with these needs interferes with normal development and encourages regressive behavior. Many of the work-saving devices by which we are surrounded increasingly eliminate man's need for physical, emotional and intellectual activity. We substitute gadgets for human contacts; ignore the potentiality for individual creativity and achievement. Human beings are thus forced into greater and greater passivity.

At this point, I would like to talk about the two scientific inventions which interfere most seriously with the healthy development of children, keeping them on an infantile level or forcing them to regress. I mean the automobile and television. To be sure, neither of these, nor any of thousands of gadgets would be harmful if they were used reasonably, if we did not allow them to dominate our lives.

The automobile replaces walking as an important physical activity. It separates people from both natural environment and human contact. What a loss for a child not to walk down a street, jump, run along a footpath, cross a vacant lot, get acquainted with other living creatures, meet a new bug, discover a flower, a new color, a new smell, talk to a bird—not to learn to reach out, to participate in the life around him; master difficulties or protect himself from danger; experience, experiment; use his energy to really learn to live.

Instead, the automobile. Children don't go anywhere on their own, they go where the car goes—on paved roads, surrounded by thousands of other cars, steel prisons carrying their prisoners. "Sit down—don't jump around—stop fighting," says the driver. "Want to get killed? Just wait till we get home! This is the last time I'll ever take you out in the car!" If only they would make good this threat!

What do the children see? Angry, frightened faces. What do they inhale? Gasoline exhaust, smog. What do they hear? Noise—unbearable, distracting. Brakes screeching, horns blowing, people yelling—sounds of danger, destruction, not sounds of life. To be sure, we can use automobiles to go places, to take the children to the beach, to the park or to the country. But how often do we do this? "Let's go for a ride," becomes a goal in itself. Just going, letting the world pass by at high speed without participating in it. Children are forced into passivity, become restless, bored—irritated and irritating, punished or exhorted to go to sleep.

The passive prisoner status ends abruptly for many on their sixteenth birthday. Then teenagers are presented with the keys to the prison. After years of enforced passivity, they react to their freedom with a vengeance. They endanger themselves and others and start preparing for their own future roles as jailers. Exaggerated? Thousands of traffic fatalities, many times that number of crippling injuries occurring month after month and year after year are not exaggerations but statistics. To say nothing about all the physical illnesses caused by physical inactivity.

Harmful as are automobiles, they are less so than television. The intense preoccupation with cars is a passing fancy for teenagers, but small children, even adults, become addicted to television. There is much criticism of television, most of it centering around the quality of the programs, the advertising, the violence, the exploitation of this powerful medium of communication for purposes not in the interest of the public good. Valid as these criticisms are, and I wholeheartedly agree with them, they are insignificant compared with the harm just watching television does to children. It keeps them on a regressed level of orality, isolates them from living human beings, and forces them into passivity at a time when physical, emotional and mental activity is even more important than later in life, when it is essential for maturation.

Feeding ready-made fantasies and ideas to growing children is like bottle-feeding them with infants' formulas. They watch activity instead of being active. They experience violent fantasies, not only because of the content of the programs but because of the passivity enforced on them by television viewing in itself. Only by their own activity can they learn to master or modify destructive impulses in themselves, learn to do creative things with their aggressive energy instead of accumulating it as a destructive and self-destructive force.

There are other ways television interferes with development. The idea that entertainment is available any time, all the time, by just pushing a button is poor training for life. In real life, we have to work for pleasures, for satisfactions. It is essential for healthy maturation that children learn to postpone, modify, change, even give up altogether some of their desires. And what does television do? Exactly the opposite. Every means of persuasion is employed to counteract what parents are trying, or should try, to teach children. They are constantly encouraged to demand more and more, to get everything they want right now. "Why just at Christmas, why not every day?"—"Have pleasure now, pay later." And they do pay later. It teaches irresponsibility and a sense of unreality. It emphasizes the most irrelevant and superficial aspects of existence.

At the same time, television dramatizes violence, pain, destructiveness, misery, while saying in effect, don't worry. All's well as long as you rely on supermen, as long as you don't offend, as long as you use the right deodorant, the right detergent, as long as there is a dove in your kitchen. Human emotions cannot compete with the vulgar exaggerations of the commercials— they are deadened by the explosions of the "Dirt Bombs."

It is difficult for parents to compete with the seductive authorities, the idealized celebrities of television. They never punish, never prohibit, never tell children to behave, to go to sleep, to stop watching television and do their homework. Children become addicted to television as adults do to stimulants, sleeping pills, alcohol. It is not surprising that so many grow up feeling that they cannot do anything for themselves and look for more and more artificial stimulation. Yet too many parents encourage, or even force children to watch television in order to keep them quiet, out of the way. Things are so much more peaceful than if children are running around, being noisy, making a mess! But television is a very poor substitute for human relationships.

## 16. Female Sexuality and Masculine Bias

The classical psychoanalytic theory of female sexual development has been under scrutiny since the early days of psychoanalysis. According to this theory, the sexual development of a girl is determined entirely by her lack of a penis, and childbirth is a substitute for the non-existent penis. There is some question as to whether Freud himself was quite satisfied with it, but his theory was founded on the faulty biological knowledge available at the time.

There is increasing evidence today that this earlier data was defective and was based upon the existing, all-pervasive masculine bias from which Freud himself, of course, was not exempt. Recent studies force the conclusion that in the human, as well as the animal world, female sexuality is primary, that life begins with the female organism and that the male, as a contributor to procreation and the development of the species, comes later. These studies demonstrate that female sexuality has always been stronger biologically than male sexuality, but that from the very beginning of civilization it was suppressed in order to establish and protect family life, the basic unit of society. (After all, Man couldn't just let Woman run around enjoying herself, flaunting her biological superiority and neglecting home and children!)

We know a great deal about penis envy. There is no question that it exists, that it is intense and is easy to observe in daily life as well as in the analysis of every woman. We also know how universal is masculine bias, demonstrated by the male's depreciation of women and belief in his own superiority—above all, in his sexual function and capability. Expressions like, "Congratulations, it's a boy!"—or, "Too bad, it's a girl. Better luck next time!"—don't need any explanation. What is only beginning to be recognized is that behind man's ambivalence toward woman is his envy of her potentially greater sexual ability and her ability to create life. It is a source of his feelings of inferiority and resentment against them.

There are good reasons also to support the premise that man's greater creativity in artistic and scientific fields is based on this envy and competitiveness. Our daily speech dealing with creativity is revealing. A man is "pregnant with" or "gives birth to" a new idea; has an "abortive thought" or a "brain-child." Very common, too, are such expressions as, "This is my creation, my baby. I thought of it first!"—and the fight over priority in this regard can be fierce among men. Furthermore, dreams and even symptoms of pregnancy are not uncommonly experienced by husbands of pregnant women. And feelings of emptiness, depression, after completing a major work are familiar to creative men and are similar to those of women after childbirth. There are many ways in which man expresses his envy of and hostility toward pregnant women—none more cruel than are demonstrated by our archaic abortion laws, which are responsible for thousands of deaths every year, for untold humiliation, suffering, life-long illness and sterility.

The history of civilization, primitive, ancient and modern, is gorged with proofs of man's envy of women and his severe ambivalence toward them. They have been mistrusted, persecuted, treated as second-rate human beings in practically every culture, even denied the right to vote until recently in the most civilized societies. They have been discriminated against in every religion. Idealization of the Virgin Mother on the one hand and centuries of denunciation as the source of all evil on the other. The witch-hunting, taboos and ceremonies of primitive societies expressing ambivalence toward women fill volumes. What about its expression in the artificial mother-culture of our own time? The highly idealized "sainted mother" who is reviled and ridiculed the moment she stops being a mother and becomes a mother-in-law.

Consider the story of Genesis, written of course by men. Genesis tells us that God created the universe—and, as His crowning achievement, created man in His own image. God, always depicted as all-powerful and male, creates the sun, moon, earth, oceans, forests, the billions of living creatures and finally, man. But man was lonely so God helped him to create the first woman out of his own body, performing the miracle of miracles, usurping the one function of woman man is unable to duplicate—the creation of life. In the same genre, is the myth about Pallas Athena springing full-grown from the head of Zeus.

Why has man never paused to analyze or explain these startling phenomena? The answer must be the same as the reason why he created these beautiful fantasies in the first place: his awe, envy and megalomaniac denial of his feelings of worthlessness in the face of woman's life-giving role. They give comfort to his shaky and injured self-esteem, feed and reinforce his masculine bias.

The subject is further complicated by the fact that women accept and identify with this bias, deprecating their role as mothers, labelling outstanding women in business or the professions as masculine and equating lesser intelligence and passivity with femininity. Yet is it not possible, for example, that the reason they do not excel in the scientific and artistic fields to the extent that men do may very well be due not to lesser capability but to lesser need to express their creativity in these directions?

Man's knowledge that he cannot create but can only destroy life has undoubtedly affected the entire course of civilization. It is reasonable to speculate whether it may not be one of the driving forces behind his incessant urge to make wars throughout history. Today, as "the father of the hydrogen bomb" he is at last in a position to threaten with destruction all life created by woman.

# PART TWO

# THE PRACTICE OF PSYCHOANALYSIS

## 17. Psychoanalysis as a Method of Treatment

Psychoanalysis is a special form of therapy suitable for the treatment of a variety of emotional disturbances, but not for all. Analysis requires a great expenditure of time, effort and money. It places responsibilities and restrictions on the patient which not everyone is capable of accepting. It should not be recommended lightly. There are emotional difficulties which are not severe enough to warrant such a drastic approach. They can be treated by other forms of psychotherapy, generally in much less time and without probing deeply into the total personality. On the other hand, there are people who are so severely disturbed that some other approach is required, at least initially.

In some cases, the analyst can determine very quickly whether psychoanalysis is indicated. In others, he may have to see a patient a number of times before arriving at a decision. The problems are similar to those doctors have to deal with in other branches of medicine. Some patients need surgery, others medications, still others a change of diet, the application of heat or cold, or no treatment at all. Sometimes it is easy to make a diagnosis, sometimes very difficult, requiring all kinds of laboratory work, x-rays, consultations.

Psychoanalysis, in a way, can be compared with the surgical, radical approach to physical medicine, with one important difference. A surgeon can put his patient to sleep and operate without his active participation. The analyst, on the contrary, must have the patient's full cooperation. The patient does not have to "believe in" psychoanalysis, any more than in medicine, surgery, or the practice of law. The best-motivated patients are those who seek help because they are unhappy, suffering, not functioning well and because they hope that analysis will benefit them. The patient's desire and ability to cooperate with the analyst, therefore, are important considerations in recommending analysis and will to a large extent determine its success or failure.

Analysts do not accept for treatment an individual who comes just because he is "curious" about psychoanalysis or wants to do some member of his family "a favor." Anyone who says, "I'm sure I don't need help, I'm only here because my husband (or wife) insists on it," is not a candidate for analysis unless the analyst recognizes that this is a thinly-veiled attempt to cover up fear or shame, to save face. Emotional illness still carries a stigma in our society, just as did tuberculosis or the "social diseases" not so long ago. It is looked upon as "weakness," especially in men.

How can one find out if one needs psychoanalysis? Certainly the best approach is to consult an accredited psychoanalyst. Often, this is easier said than done, because so many people don't know how to go about finding one. A good way is to consult the nearest Psychoanalytic Society. The American Psychoanalytic Association now has 28 affiliated Societies throughout the country and the number increases steadily. The majority of their members practice in the city where the Society is located, but some may practice in neighboring communities, or even at quite a distance away. If you have the name of an analyst in mind, the Society can tell you whether he is an accredited member. If not, it can give you the names of several analysts in good standing.

Or you might ask your family physician to recommend someone. This may or may not turn out well, depending on how the physician feels about psychoanalysis. The majority of patients today are referred to analysts by their physicians, but unfortunately, there are still too many doctors who are either misinformed about psychoanalysis and psychoanalysts, or are strongly opposed to the idea of any psychiatric treatment and will tell you that "you're crazy to think of such a thing . . . forget it . . . it's all in your mind."

The question still remains, why should one consider consulting a psychoanalyst in the first place? Symptoms of emotional disturbance can be very outspoken. Prolonged depression, serious work inhibition, severe anxiety, impotence in men, frigidity in women, frequent or disabling physical illnesses without organic cause are good reasons for consulting a psychoanalyst.

The problem is greater when the symptoms are not so obvious. There are people who complain of mild physical symptoms year after year and go from doctor to doctor for check-ups which reveal nothing. They consume quantities of vitamins, tranquilizers, stimulants and sleeping pills; take thyroid, try the mountains or the seashore; go from job to job, from marriage to marriage, and always find something or someone else to blame for their problems. These are people who live in constant fear of failure, yet frequently behind this fear is the unrecognized greater fear of success.

Then there are the people who are always lonely, whether they are alone or surrounded by people they know. They crave a meaningful relationship with another human being, a friend, a mate, a sexual partner, but never succeed in establishing one. There are people with all kinds of potentials who somehow manage to waste their energies, their abilities, their very lives. Many of these could benefit from psychoanalysis. Some do finally seek help, after years of hesitation, sometimes so late that all that is left for them is to look back on decades of wasted living. Some never do, out of ignorance, or guilt, or shame, or because they don't know how to go about it.

The question is asked frequently whether psychoanalysis can benefit children as well as adults. One of the cornerstones of psychoanalytic theory is that the first few years of life are of the utmost importance in the development of every individual. They mold our characters, determine how well or how poorly we will function later, influence our ability to establish satisfactory relationships with others, affect the choice of our friends, our life partners, establish our attitudes toward pleasure, work, responsibilities.

Growth is a natural process but it is difficult even under favorable conditions, and emotional disturbances are not unusual during childhood. Many of these disturbances subside without requiring special treatment. In some instances, a discussion of the problem with a parent may be sufficient. But sometimes serious emotional illnesses occur. These may require intense, lengthy therapy, and for certain conditions psychoanalysis is the best approach. There are many excellent child therapists within and outside the medical profession, and some psychoanalysts specialize in child analysis. There are also excellent clinics for treating emotionally disturbed children. Pediatricians, family physicians, schoolteachers and administrators are increasingly conscious of these problems when they arise, and they are generally the ones who advise parents to seek help for their children.

Psychoanalysts certainly do not maintain that everyone can benefit from psychoanalysis. It is a tool for the treatment of people who are sick— who cannot function, or who function under such tension that their lives are a constant torment. Even then, the analyst must determine not only whether the disturbance is severe enough to warrant such a major undertaking but whether it is of a nature that can be helped by analysis.

He must also take into consideration whether the individual is in a position to devote the necessary time. If circumstances make this impossible, then of course the treatment cannot be undertaken. Furthermore, it is a prerequisite that the individual must have some freedom of choice in his life situation. He cannot analyze someone who is in a concentration camp, or in Death Row, or about to go into combat. He may talk to him and relieve him of some anxiety but he cannot analyze him because his life situation is circumscribed. There are other limitations, other unchangeable situations such as severe physical handicaps or chronic illnesses which make analysis inadvisable.

Nor do analysts decide on the basis of

diagnostic labels alone whether or not a patient is suitable for analysis. The more we learn about the human mind, about mental structure and mental illness, the less we are able to draw sharp lines between neurosis, psychosis and character disturbance. There are many psychoanalysts who work with psychotics with good results. On the other hand, there are patients who are difficult or impossible to analyze even though they are diagnosed as neurotics or as suffering from character disorders.

Psychoanalysis is a lengthy procedure and any treatment requiring a great deal of time is expensive. These are practical drawbacks. However, there are also many physical illnesses which require even longer treatment and are far more costly. Certain skin diseases, allergies, orthopedic conditions, deformities resulting from injuries, infantile paralysis, neurological diseases, arthritis, kidney diseases, heart diseases, diabetes, infections like tuberculosis, take years, sometimes even life-long treatment in and out of hospitals.

Analysts find that the optimum time for an analytic session is about one hour. The number of sessions per week may vary but the majority of patients are seen four or five times a week for two to four years, sometimes even longer. Why does it take so long? Psychoanalysis does not deal with anything as specific as removing an inflamed appendix or setting a broken bone. It deals with the total life and functioning of the patient. It concerns itself with the present; the remembered and forgotten past; the conscious thoughts and feelings; the fantasies; the area of the Unconscious, the unknown and buried part of the personality.

Psychoanalysis must help the patient to achieve self-knowledge and there is nothing more laborious than the process of learning to see ourselves as we really are, not as we think we are or as we think we ought to be. It must deal with the patient's disturbed relationships with those close to him and with society. It must help him to re-evaluate his attitudes, misconceptions, fears, hopes, strivings. It is a process of maturation, difficult enough in the normal course of growing up, but infinitely more so when it has been delayed and blocked for whatever reasons.

For a child, the whole world consists of the few important figures in the family—first the mother, then the other members. It takes a long time before a patient begins to realize that the adult world does not have to be an enlarged facsimile of his childhood world, before he can accept the fact that many new worlds are open to him if he is prepared to enter them. But how difficult it is to change lifelong, rigid attitudes, to convince oneself that one does not have to be bound by endless, painful repetitions of the past which have long since lost their validity.

Those who look upon the world as if it

were a small room with mirrors for walls, in which they see their own reflections endlessly, have to be helped to realize that they can break the mirrors and open windows and doors into wide new worlds of choices and opportunities. At the same time, they must come to recognize and accept their limitations, must learn to function and live satisfactorily with them instead of driving toward unattainable goals leading inevitably to frustration and failure. They must learn to accept, too, the fact that pleasure and pain, success and failure are part of everyone's life.

To bring about these changes in the personality takes a great deal of time and the analyst who would help his patient must proceed slowly, just as an orthopedic surgeon does when he tries to mobilize a rigid joint stiffened by a chronic disease. Forcing matters too quickly, both the surgeon and the analyst can do more harm than good.

## 18. The Analytic Situation

Before an analysis can be undertaken, specific arrangements must be agreed upon by both analyst and patient as to the hour of the day to be reserved, the frequency of sessions and the fee to be charged. The analyst obligates himself to keep the time agreed upon available and the patient agrees to accept responsibility for the appointed time. The analyst also suggests that the patient try to arrange his vacation to coincide with his own. Since he is usually able to give the patient plenty of advance notice, this rarely presents a problem.

If the patient is an adult, he must personally accept the responsibility of paying the analyst. This is sometimes difficult for an individual who has not been accustomed to handling his own financial affairs. A wife may say that her husband has always paid the bills and that he will be angry if this arrangement is upset, only to find that her fears are groundless and that the husband may even be pleased that she accepts the responsibility.

Obviously, it is unnecessary for an analyst

who sees a patient almost every day to mail him a bill at the end of the month, when he can just hand it to him. It is just as unnecessary for the patient to mail the analyst a check. Some analysts never give the patient a bill. They expect the patient to keep track of what he owes and to pay them directly at the end of the month. There are good reasons for this realistic procedure. Patients express all kinds of attitudes, conscious and unconscious, within the analytic situation by the way they handle the payment of the analyst's fees. These help the analyst to learn certain things about the patient and eventually help the patient to learn not only how he feels about money, but also how he uses it to express conflicts and feelings which have nothing to do with money.

There are some patients who forget my name every time they write a check. Some forget to sign the check, or date it years ahead. One who owed me $100. sent me a check for $100,000., which served his purpose as well as if he had given me nothing. A patient may carefully make out a check at home, put it in a coat pocket or purse, and then select another coat or purse to wear to the analytic session. Another may say he has no pen. If I point to the pen on my desk, he may tell me he doesn't want to waste my time, or that he can't make it out in my presence. One may bring a check in a fully-addressed envelope and put it carefully on my desk, while another practically throws it at me on his way in or out of the office. All of these actions have important meanings. They are characteristic for each individual and have to be dealt with in the analytic situation.

Every analyst makes sure that his office affords quiet and privacy. Noise interferes with thinking and with listening. What is more, the patient has to feel assured of absolute privacy, must know that whatever is said in this office will go no further. Anyone who has ever been in analysis knows that there are times when the patient does not believe this, no matter how much we reassure him. If he hears a muffled sound from an outside corridor, he is sure someone is listening.

People are surprised when they learn that analysts' offices generally have separate entrances and exits. The reason is simple. There are many patients who are ashamed of their emotional difficulties and do not want to be seen coming or going. Analysts respect this feeling. It is the patient's privilege to want this privacy although usually, as the analysis progresses, it no longer troubles him.

Generally, after one or more interviews, the analyst requests the patient to lie down on the couch. Again, as with the payment of fees, no two patients react in the same way. There are those who come to the office for the first time and immediately head for the couch. Others are terrified of the idea and act as if they don't know how to get there. Some keep one foot on the ground as though ready to take off. Some fluff up the pillow, take off their shoes, straighten every seam before they lie down. Some lie rigidly; others curl up, all set to go to sleep.

Why the couch? Nothing mysterious about it. It is simply a tool used in the interest of both patient and analyst. It is the primary task of the analysis to uncover and bring to light the repressed, unconscious conflicts, thoughts, fantasies and feelings which have so profoundly affected the life and functioning of the patient without his knowledge.

The method which psychoanalysis has found to be most constructive for dredging up unconscious material by the patient is called "free association." The patient is requested to lie back on the couch and to express spontaneously every thought and feeling which flows through his mind, just as it occurs to him, no matter how unimportant, embarrassing, painful, indiscreet or senseless it seems to him. Nothing is to be omitted or edited or substituted. Lying down where he cannot see the analyst (who is seated out of view, behind the head of the couch) he is likely to be more relaxed and can talk more freely than if he were constantly watching the analyst's face for his reactions.

The analyst, too, is freer out of sight

of his patient to concentrate on listening and piecing together the meaning of what is being produced. From his position, he is also able to observe the facial expressions, gestures and movements of the patient, which are frequently as revealing as the words being spoken.

Early in the analysis, the analyst explains that especially in the beginning, he will listen much more than he will talk, because he must learn a great deal about the patient before he can be helpful. He prepares the patient for the fact that he will ask all kinds of questions which the analyst may or may not answer—not because he does not wish to but because questions are a part of free association, too, and it is important for the analyst to understand the reasons which motivate the questions.

Through free association, we bring together ideas, thoughts and feelings that belong together even though we have lost track of the connections. Piecing together the free associations, it eventually becomes clear that certain attitudes, fears, feelings affecting our present lives are inevitably linked with childhood experiences. Even though these early meanings have been lost, we have continued to live with them as if they were still valid.

The patient starting analysis agrees that he will do his best to permit his thoughts and feelings to flow without inhibition, but soon finds that it is very difficult to do. Frequently throughout the analysis, free associations become blocked by anxiety, guilt or shame, which the analyst must help him to work through before he can go on. It is almost as if there were three people in the analytic situation—an adult who comes for help, the analyst who seeks to understand, to help, and a third person, an anxious child or irrational self who warns: "Don't tell him . . . watch out . . . be careful . . . this is dangerous . . . painful . . . he will hurt you."

Nevertheless, the patient who can overcome his resistances, eventually succeeds, helped by the interpretations of the analyst, in bringing to consciousness and resolving the unconscious conflicts which have held him in a vise and impeded his growth.

## 19. The Transference Phenomenon

Psychoanalysis maintains that emotional illnesses are rooted in infantile sources which have been repressed and are therefore unconscious and unknown to us. The goal of analysis is to bring them into the open, to make them conscious, so that the patient may gain insight into how these unconscious forces have distorted his development and his relationships to others. The transference phenomenon is of crucial importance in achieving this goal.

Transference means that in the course of the analysis, the patient transfers onto the analyst all the emotions—fear, anger, need, desire, love, hate, envy and so on—which he experienced knowingly and unknowingly toward important figures in his early childhood. Not only are the feelings transferred, but upon the neutral person of the analyst, whatever his sex or age, the patient superimposes significant figures of his early life, so that on one occasion or another the analyst will represent an authoritarian father, a loving mother, a hated brother or sister, grandmother, uncle, etc. The feelings of the long-buried past come alive again in the analytic situation, in all their original intensity, and are experienced as if they have present-day validity in relation to the analyst. To put it another way, the patient actually relives his entire neurosis in the analytic setting.

To be sure, transferred feelings are not confined to the analytic setting. They occur to some degree in all human relationships. The difference is that outside the analysis, the patient can act on these feelings and, automatically, those toward whom he directs his actions will react. Within the analytic situation, he experiences these emotions and talks about them, but cannot act on them. Furthermore, the analyst, cognizant of what is going on, does not react personally, as he very well might with anyone who is not a patient. Instead, it is his task to analyze these transferred emotions with his patient and to trace them back to their original source.

It is because the transference situation is so vital in the treatment of the patient that the analyst must maintain a neutral, objective relationship with him. The less the patient knows about the analyst as a real person, the easier it will be to fantasy about him during the analysis, and the more suitable the analyst will be to represent the various transference figures. That is why psychoanalysts do not analyze their friends and why social contact between patient and analyst is avoided. There is a great difference between feeling loved or hated, rejected or punished by someone we do not know or by someone who is close to us.

The need to preserve the privacy and confidential nature of an analysis also creates problems with the family, and sometimes even with the referring physician, who resents all the secrecy about a patient he has treated for years. The family, of course, is anxious, feels excluded, would like to know what is going on and is eager to volunteer all kinds of information. This is perfectly understandable, and sometimes it may even be helpful to talk to a relative, but the analyst must make it clear that he will not do so without his patient's knowledge and that he will not discuss anything that goes on in the analytic setting.

The analyst does not have to do anything to help the transference develop—it does so spontaneously out of the patient's need and the analytic situation—but he must avoid doing anything which will interfere. This he accomplishes by establishing an analytic atmosphere, which means that he preserves a neutral, non-critical, non-directive attitude, indicating neither approval nor disapproval of the patient's words and actions. He does not tell the patient what to do and what not to do in conducting his life, unless his actions may result in serious injury to himself or others.

It is not easy always to maintain a neutral attitude, to resist reassuring or advising a patient who suffers and, sometimes, the analyst yields— although he knows that in the long run, yielding to the dependency need of the patient merely delays his progress toward independence.

The feelings expressed by the patient reflect his internal conflicts and the analyst must remain an objective arbitrator. Of course the analyst does have feelings about what is going on, and sometimes these are his best clues to understanding what the patient is trying unconsciously to convey. The analyst, for example, finds that he is reacting with feelings of pity, guilt, confusion, etc., and recognizes that for some reason this is exactly what the patient wants. Or he may feel irritated by something the patient has said, then realizes that the patient may be doing it in order to provoke punishment. Whatever his reactions, however, the analyst uses them to understand and to help the patient understand the underlying meaning of his feelings and actions.

Sometimes, the patient may see the analyst as the most powerful person in the world, the greatest, the kindest; at other times, as the most hateful, the most cruel. One day he feels grateful to the analyst because he feels well. The next day he will blame him for a headache or a quarrel with his wife or his employer. In the course of a day, an analyst may hear:

"You are too short."

"You are so old."

"You look so much younger today."

"You are very attractive."

"You are too fat."

"You are very ugly."

"You look angry."

"You look depressed."

To what extent these reactions are distortions under the influence of the past is easy to demonstrate. All I have to do is to ask the patient, while on the couch, to tell me what I look like. Often a patient will find it impossible to recall any of my features, or with great conviction will describe me as a foot taller or shorter than I am— or twenty pounds heavier or lighter. One may insisit that I always wear white socks and that he dislikes my striped suit. Of course I have never worn either. Obviously, the patient is describing someone in his past, and from his description it is easy to point out how he really feels about this person and how he has transferred these feelings to me, the analyst, just as he transfers unconscious feelings from his past into his other present-day relationships.

For whatever reasons, there are more people in our society who are afraid of loving than of hating. They talk about love, crave it, but fear it. "I'm afraid of being hurt . . . of being rejected," is expressed in words or in a variety of actions. Anger, hate, seem safer; they keep people at a distance and are easier to justify.

The goal of analysis is to help a patient to become aware of his feelings and to be able to express them in words rather than actions. The more freely they are expressed, the less the patient will act on them in or out of the analysis, the easier it becomes to trace the origin of the transference feelings to early childhood relationships. Expressions of the transference contribute to the understanding of the unconscious conflicts. As the analysis progresses and comes to a successful conclusion, the transference is resolved and the analyst once again becomes to the patient not a figure in his fantasies but the physician he was when the analysis began, a person to whom he will be grateful for having helped him.

From what I have described about transference, about the interplay of feelings between patient and analyst, it should be clear why the training of psychoanalysts has to be so exacting and why not all who apply are accepted for training. It should be obvious also why they themselves must undergo intensive analysis.

Admission Committees may not always agree on every detail, but there are certain criteria which are universally considered desirable. Some feel that only mature people should be considered for training. I prefer to say that we look for people who show a potential for maturity in the course of their own analysis. It is desirable that they have enough inner freedom to fantasy, to have day dreams. The so-called absolutely normal people are the most difficult to deal with. They have learned to behave in ways which in our society are looked upon as normal functioning. They are successful in their professions as well as in other fields. Yet, when we look closer, we find that they have never been able to sustain an intense, satisfactory relationship with anyone, because they can maintain their "normalcy" only so long as they can keep their distance, hang on rigidly to their defenses.

We look for individuals who have the capacity to suffer as well to experience joy. They must be endowed with empathy, the ability to project themselves into the other fellow's shoes, to feel his suffering as well as to understand it intellectually. Psychoanalysts have to live with social and personal restrictions not required in other branches of medicine or in other professions. We look for people who willingly accept this limitation.

A prerequisite for practicing psychoanalysis is the ability to withstand the insistence of patients that they are suffering and must have immediate relief. The temptation to do something quickly is very great, but an analyst must have the strength to be patient, the self-control to hold back and wait for the right time to help. Anyone who does not have this stubborn patience and control should not be an analyst, although he might very well be good at some other form of therapy.

We look for individuals who can deal with aggression, their own as well as that of their patients. They have to have learned to deal with their conflicts in their own analysis and to understand how to use them constructively. Otherwise, they will not help but may even do harm, either by wrong actions or by being too passive in the analytic situation.

## 20. The Use of Dreams

Freud spent many years analyzing dreams and their meanings before publishing his first major work on psychoanalysis, "The Interpretation of Dreams," in 1900. These studies led him to the discovery of the existence of the Unconscious and to an understanding of its workings. He considered this work to be his most significant contribution to the understanding of human psychology.

From his investigations, Freud concluded that dreams are not haphazard, confused creations of the mind but that they are the result of a psychic mechanism which he called the dreamwork, and that they have meaning and purpose. Furthermore, he demonstrated that if we understand the dreamwork, we can explain and interpret the real meaning of dreams. He stated also that, by and large, dreams represent the fulfillment of unconscious wishes which serve to protect the dreamer's sleep.

If we consider the dreams of young children, the fact that they represent wish-fulfillments is easy to perceive. A sleepy child asks for a piece of candy. The mother refuses to give it to him in spite of all his protests. He goes to bed frustrated, full of conflict. Even after he falls asleep, the conflict continues, disturbing his sleep. So the dream comes to the rescue and finds a solution. The child dreams that he has all the candy he could wish for, the wish is fulfilled and he continues to sleep peacefully.

Adult dreams are not as easy to understand. The way we remember and describe a dream is called the *manifest dream*. It makes an interesting story but generally does not reveal the real meaning of the dream. Only through the process of dream interpretation in analytic therapy do we arrive at the underlying or *latent dream content*.

A dream is usually triggered by something which occurred during the preceding day. (This is called the *day residue*.) It might have been something seemingly innocuous which hardly attracted our waking attention, yet it evoked from the past an unconscious desire or a repressed conflict trying to find a solution in our dream. Physical sensations, pain, may stimulate dreams also, but they do not explain them. Whether the stimulation comes from a headache, a stomach ache, a need to urinate, to wake up, the form and meaning of the dream will depend on what the dreamer does with it.

In dreams, two conflicting forces seek to

141

find a compromise. An unconscious need is trying to break through and find satisfaction, and the other force, which is called the *dream censor,* tries to prevent this. To some degree, and in disguised form, censorship persists even in our sleep, but because we are immobilized and cannot act, the censorship relaxes enough to permit the Ego to find solutions for our conflicts in our dreams.

It may be well at this point to mention that one of the great dangers of stimulants, particularly of LSD, is that the same feelings, desires, conflicts which fill our dreams are experienced under the influence of LSD, but at a time when we are not immobilized by sleep. There is no danger to us if we dream that we are flying, but if we are convinced that we can fly when we are not asleep, as happens frequently to people taking LSD, then we may actually fly off the roof of a skyscraper.

In contrast to our thinking when we are awake, what we see in our dreams are expressions of what is called *primary process thinking.* There are all kinds of actions in dreams which may not represent actions at all, but substitutes for feelings or thoughts, comparable to the technique used in silent films or in pantomime. Some of the characteristics of primary process thinking are the following:

(1) Symbols are taken literally. They do not represent something symbolically, they are

the thing itself. For example, any symbol for the penis—a sharp instrument, a cigar—is the penis itself. A house is not a symbol for Mother, but Mother herself.

(2) In this primary process, there are no contradictions, and totally contradictory forces exist simultaneously without being in conflict with each other, such as love and hate, masculine and feminine desires.

(3) There is no sense of time. A whole lifetime can transpire in a dream within a few seconds. (This happens sometimes in waking life, too. Faced with sudden danger, one's entire life can be re-lived in a few seconds.)

The dream-work consists of various processes. The censor, for example, interpolates conditions under which it permits an unconscious wish to find expression. If it is a wish that is strongly prohibited, the censor will permit its expression if it is couched in a less objectionable, less recognizable form. One such process is called *condensation*. By combining the characteristics of two or more people in our dream, we create one person who is a composite of all of them and who can represent any or several of them at the same time.

Another process is called *displacement*, by means of which we can express a desire which is prohibited in relation to one person, by displacing the desire onto some other person in our dream. A wish can also be displaced from one part of the body to another, and from one place to another.

Still another process is the use of *symbols* in dreams. There are many popular notions about dream symbols and what they represent, but they are generally not related to psychoanalytic thinking. Contrary to popular belief, dream symbols do not predict the future. They are of great value, however, in guiding the analyst toward correct interpretation of underlying, unconscious forces seeking expression.

Dreams are not stories. People make stories out of them when they relate them, in an effort to make their dreams sound sensible. This is what is called the *secondary process,* the thinking or intellectual process. Even though it is not deliberate, the patient is usually aware of a desire to tell his dream in such a way as to make it more acceptable. Patients also forget dreams frequently which they are making every effort to remember. These tendencies are just as much the work of the censor as the dream-work itself.

Actually, remembering dreams is not the purpose of dreaming. Its purpose is to maintain sleep by solving insoluble conflicts. If it serves this function, it serves no purpose to remember the dream. The reasons for forgetting dreams are the same as for dreaming in the first place: we dream in order to express something during sleep which we must forget or repress when we are awake.

Anxiety dreams and nightmares seem to contradict the idea that the function of dreams is to solve conflicts, to fulfill wishes in order to maintain sleep. In anxiety dreams, we often wake up. One explanation is that there are wishes which are so unacceptable to us that even in dreams we cannot find a solution for them.

In analysis, we interpret dreams through the patient's free associations. These, combined with the analyst's knowledge of the patient's problems, life situation, predominant Ego defenses, Superego, will lead to an understanding of the latent dream content. Even the use of certain symbols may be specific for an individual.

When we sleep, we withdraw from the world. Even if we dream about world problems or about other people, we are primarily seeking solutions for ourselves in our dreams. It is important to realize that the dreamer is the writer, producer, actor and director of his dream. Whoever the people are in his dream, he put them there. Whatever their characters, he invented them. Whatever they do, he makes them do. If he rescues someone from great danger, the question is how did this person get into such a dangerous situation in the first place. Why did the dreamer put him there?

If we wish to understand dreams, we

must first of all accept the fact that whatever happens in them, we are their creators. If we dream that people are doing terrible things to us, it may be our wish to prove that we are being mistreated and that therefore our anger toward these people is justified.

We do not dream about conflicts which we are able to solve in our waking lives. If we do, then the apparent reality situation is merely a springboard for other, more buried conflicts surfacing in our dream.

Today, dream interpretation is still an important part of analytic technique, but it is only a part and not as crucially significant as in the early days of psychoanalysis. Equally important, and sometimes even more helpful, depending on the patient, is the analysis of the Ego defenses and, first and foremost, the analysis of the transference.

## 21. Realistic and Unrealistic Expectations

Far more often than not, patients embarking on analysis look to it to work miracles. The analyst is a magician who will solve all their problems and fulfill all their expectations, no matter how unrealistic. In this they are of course doomed to disappointment, as they discover for themselves in the course of the analysis.

It is realistic for patients to expect that if they are suffering from crippling anxiety or depression, from all manner of painful symptoms which interfere with their functioning, analysis should rid them of these symptoms and make it possible for them to function satisfactorily in their work and in their personal lives. Of course they are disappointed when it doesn't happen quickly, what with all the current emphasis on miracle drugs promising immediate relief from all symptoms. It is easy to start with these panaceas and difficult to get rid of them. All too frequently they don't fulfill what they promise and result in increasing intolerance to pain and in thousands of drug addicts.

Psychoanalysts tell their patients that

there will be times during analysis when they may feel worse than when they started. As patients begin to dig into the roots of their disturbances, their protective defenses are loosened, their anxiety becomes temporarily greater, their symptoms worse. Of all the agonies which afflict the human mind, none is more terrifying than the shadows which govern our lives because we don't know who we are and don't understand what we feel. Just as a surgeon who is operating cannot stop cutting because there is bleeding, so the analyst cannot stop trying to get to the bottom of the pathological defenses which have distorted the patient's life, even if it hurts.

However, analysts hear less about the realistic expectations of their patients than about those which can never be fulfilled and which hark back to early childhood fantasies that parents can do anything—that if they suffer pain, their parents can alleviate it and will do so if they love their children. There are patients who say: "I don't expect to have any more problems once I am analyzed." Obviously, this wish cannot be gratified. Actually, one may have to deal with more problems after one is free of neurotic fears and prohibitions. Life is full of problems, and the better one functions, the more one must be prepared to face realistic difficulties.

There are patients who expect that once they are analyzed, they will have no responsibilities. This universal wish-fantasy to function once again under the pleasure principle of early life accounts for the common misconception that psychoanalysis encourages irresponsibility. Exactly the opposite is true. Psychoanalysis promotes maturity, and the more mature we are, the more we are capable of accepting responsibility for our own actions, and the stronger our feelings of responsibility toward those close to us and toward society.

The desire for continuous happiness is another unrealistic expectation, also based on the pleasure principle. The best to be hoped for is that one will function satisfactorily, including the ability to accept both success and failure, happiness and unhappiness.

There are patients who seriously hope that psychoanalysis will help them to get rid of their feelings altogether. They are afraid to love or hate, afraid of being hurt, punished, rejected. They long for a state of non-feeling, where nothing will ever trouble them again. Of course this is neither possible nor desirable. If the analysis is successful, it will help rid patients of excessive or inappropriate feelings. The goal may be described as having the right feelings, in the right place, at the right time, and in the right proportion. Since no one is perfect, this can never be achieved completely but analysis aims at approximating this desirable state of affairs.

One of the most unrealistic expectations is that the analyst will teach a patient *how* to feel in a given situation. This is based on centuries of unrealistically forcing on children standards of how they should and should not feel in every situation. Patients are terrified if their feelings do not conform to the expected standards. One of the most hopeless questions a patient can ask is, "How am I supposed to feel?"

Society has the right to expect that adults should be able to control most of their actions. The more mature we are, the more we should be able to do so. But we cannot control our feelings. We can fear them, deny them, repress them, but we cannot change them or produce them on order. We are taught all our lives that we must love our parents, brothers, sisters, neighbors. The result is that we feel terribly guilty if we don't love them, or if we actually also hate them.

Some people undertake analysis in the hope that it will help to end a marriage; others, to save a marriage. Neither is the goal of analysis. The goal is to help people eliminate the conflicts which interfere with their judgment, their ability to act, to recognize that everyone has choices and that they must accept responsibility for their choices. If a marriage is based entirely on a severe neurotic need and the need is eliminated, there is nothing left of the relationship. If, however, the marriage is based on something more solid, and the neurotic difficulties which interfere with it are eliminated, it can only result in a better one.

Still another expectation common to many patients is that the analyst will know what they ought to do in every situation and will advise them accordingly. Of course this is not true. Analysts place the responsibility on the patient for all his actions and do not interfere. The only exception to this rule is that if the patient is about to do something dangerous to himself or to others—and if all interpretations of his unconscious motivations fail to dissuade him—then the analyst must point out the dangers and even insist that the patient must not act. Even within the analytic setting itself, although patients are encouraged to express everything they think and feel, they are never encouraged to act on their feelings.

To repeat, then: Psychoanalysis is primarily a non-directive approach. *Within the framework of the psychoanalytic setting,* whatever his own standards may be, the analyst cannot be a judge, cannot concern himself with right and wrong. He must concern himself with causes and effects. He acts as an arbitrator between two conflicting forces in human beings. One force drives for satisfaction of desires, the other prohibits. Only a trained observer can look at both sides of the picture and try to bring order out of chaos. Psychoanalysis aims to remove the blocks which interfere with normal maturation. If it succeeds, then belatedly, the patient matures, even though it may be 10, 20, even 30 years late.

Whether this belated maturation is considered a successful outcome will depend on the individuals involved. Obviously, if a man of thirty undergoes analysis whose main problem has been that he could not function as an adult, the analysis is successful if he develops into a mature individual. He will think so and so will the analyst. His parents who, however unconsciously, may have preferred to have him remain a dependent child, will complain that the analysis has ruined their son.

Mature people, by and large, have realistic expectations about life. They strive for goals which are attainable. If our expectations far exceed our actual capacities, then we are doomed to perpetual dissatisfaction with ourselves. If we are attracted only to men and women who are unattainable, then we must resign ourselves to inevitable and lifelong loneliness.

Of course psychoanalysis is not always successful, but having been a physician for thirty-seven years, and having practiced surgery and obstetrics before becoming a psychoanalyst, I would say that it compares favorably with the results in other branches of medicine. Furthermore, just as an orthopedic surgeon, treating severe injuries or deformities, may not know for years if his treatment will be successful, so analysts do not know either. It is easier to gather statistics about broken bones that have mended than about people who have been successfully analyzed and who are able to lead a satisfactory life.

# EPILOGUE

## *ECCE HOMO!*

# EPILOGUE: *ECCE HOMO!*

Fantasies of world destruction have existed throughout civilization, but this is the first time in the history of man that the possibility of total destruction has become a reality.

Freud, discussing his theory of aggression in "An Outline of Psychoanalysis" (published in 1940, shortly after his death) said:

"Thus it may in general be suspected that the *individual* dies of his internal conflicts but that the *species* dies of its unsuccessful struggle against the external world, if the latter changes in a fashion which cannot be adequately dealt with by the adaptations which the species has acquired."

Has the human species reached this state? Has man, by means of his intellectual endowments, brought about changes in the external world which are beyond his capacity for adaptation? Throughout recorded time, man has been terrified of the forces of nature and the violence of his fellow men. Civilization represents the sum total of his efforts to assure the security and safety of the individual, by harnessing and mastering the forces of nature, and by employing various means to protect the individual from the violence of other human beings. However, man has thus far been more successful in subduing the destructive forces of nature than in modifying his own destructive instincts. Our insistent demand for more and more physical scientists has been rewarded with the creation of more and more destructive capabilities. Thirty-eight years ago, in "Civilization and Its Discontents," Freud, referring to his theory of the two forces dominating human behavior, the love instinct and the death instinct, wrote:

"The fateful question for the human species seems to me to be whether and to what extent their cultural development will succeed in mastering the disturbance of their communal life by the human instinct of aggression and self-destruction. It may be that in this respect precisely the present time deserves a special interest. Men have gained control over the forces of nature to such an extent that with their help they would have no difficulty in exterminating one another to the last man. They know this and hence comes a large part of their current unrest, their unhappiness and their mood of anxiety. And now it is to be expected that the other of the two 'Heavenly Powers',* eternal Eros, will make an effort to

*From one of the Harp-Player's songs in Goethe's "Wilhelm Meister."

assert himself in the struggle with his equally immortal adversary. But who can foresee with what success and with what result?"

These words were written at the beginning of the Hitler horror but long before the atomic age, when man's destructive potential has reached unimaginable heights. Yet, grave as is the danger of atomic holocaust, this is only one aspect of the dangers confronting humanity. There is a constantly increasing distance between man's rapidly developing intellect and his unchanging emotions. The tension between intellect and emotion has been growing over the centuries, never more rapidly than during the past few decades. In our technological society, there is ever-accelerating appreciation, encouragement and reward of intellectual attainments, while at the same time there is depreciation and denial of human emotions and emotional needs, with the exception of violence.

Human beings cannot function without the satisfaction of emotional needs. Feelings are what make life worth living, and feelings are also the source of all our anxiety, all our unhappiness. Yet, to talk about feelings seems "unscientific" today, when science is so concerned with computers, machines, chemical formulas, new drugs, tranquilizers, substances which increase the memory of the rat in the hope that it will do the same for men. But to what end?

What is the result of the dichotomy

between the unchangeable feelings, needs, drives of human beings and the technical achievements created by the human brain? These achievements are supposed to serve human security, human needs. Instead, they serve only to increase our insecurity and our anxiety, while our capacity to annihilate civilization expands from moment to moment with no end in sight.

There are two vital essentials for healthy human development and functioning: satisfactory relations with other human beings and meaningful activity. Anything which interferes with these needs encourages and increases the use of man's aggressive energy for violent and destructive ends. Our scientific advances work against both these needs, tend to further isolate people from one another and to force them into passivity.

Isolation is encouraged from the very moment of birth. Immediately after birth, in most hospitals, babies are separated from their mothers and carried off to more "hygienic" surroundings. To be born, to experience the first impact of the outer world, to have to take that first breath to survive, is quite a shock, and only the mother's warmth, physical and emotional, can give the newborn infant the feeling that the world outside the womb does not merely represent pain and danger, but comfort, reassurance, trust.

Why the separation? Sterility has been crowned king. The discovery of bacteria, the

L. u. 23
29
25
2.4

29
30
37

35 - 40

45

01

Kiplinger's Personal Finance
Magazine December issue

achievements of Pasteur and Lister, the use of antiseptics, have eliminated untold suffering, saved millions of lives. But if we exaggerate their usefulness to the exclusion of emotional needs, we can nullify their value and do more harm than good.

Instead of using the creations of our intellect for our benefit, we have increasingly become their slaves—working like slaves the greatest part of our lives to achieve "a higher standard of living." The average American, we are told, invests more money in automobiles than he ever does in a home, yet children must be raised in a home, wherever procreation may occur.

It is in the nature of machines, that once we produce them, they begin producing each other. One of the greatest of all industries is the machine tool industry, which makes machines to make machines. As our knowledge has grown, so machines have grown more powerful, more complicated till they can replace complex human activities and diminish the importance of human beings altogether. Machines are a threat to human beings because they can make human effort obsolete and because their power automatically increases man's ability to destroy.

In the beginning, man used his hands, his bare fists to fight. Then he learned to throw stones, shoot arrows, use dynamite, and now finally atomic energy. Even in war, men are increasingly being separated from other men. The time is long past when a general could say, "Don't shoot till you can see the whites of their eyes." With the possible exception of guerrilla fighting, people kill without seeing each other, the distances are too great. It need not even require human effort, pushing a button can do the job.

What is more, with all our technical know-how about food production, millions continue to starve, not only because of population growth but because we use food as a weapon and because with machines we can destroy more food in a few hours than thousands of people can grow it or destroy it in many months by human effort alone.

With our advances in biology, chemistry, physiology, we have learned a great deal about the functioning of the human body. What's the result? More anxiety. We worry about eating too much protein, too little protein, too many carbohydrates, not enough minerals, vitamins, etc. We are afraid to be skinny, afraid to be fat. We feel guilty about the normal enjoyment of food and our anxieties create more problems than the foods we are afraid of.

We have moon rockets to take us into space, and intercontinental missiles to destroy the earth we live on. We create miracles with our chemical knowledge and by the same token poison the air we breathe, the food we eat, the water we drink. We have invented the miracle of television but use it far more to exploit man's passion for violence and to interfere with the development of our children than to promote education and the enjoyment of our cultural heritage.

With what we have learned about bacteriology and chemistry, we have eradicated diseases which have killed millions of people for centuries. Now we bring this same knowledge to the possible destruction of millions with chemical and bacteriological warfare.

Our knowledge constantly increases our life expectancy, but all it does is to increase the number of years we live as old people, with all sorts of restrictions on useful and gainful activity. We mature at the same period of our lives as we always did, and we become middle-aged at the same time as before. We put a premium on youth and in many industries refuse employment even to the middle-aged. In any case, these advances can only maintain our physical being. It is fascinating to see an artificial heart and before long, we will have artificial hearts, lungs and kidneys which will be able to maintain life perhaps for decades, while the patient remains unconscious. But is this living?

War used to be considered part of the natural order of things, in order to eliminate the weak and insure the survival of the fit. I question whether this was ever true, but even if it were, our technical know-how has reversed the process. Now we protect the weak, the unfit, and use the strongest, most fit, to kill and be killed, or to be crippled for life. We are very proud of the fact that few of our soldiers now die on the battlefield. The great advances in transportation and medicine save their lives, their physical lives. I have seen too many of these survivors who hate doctors for the rest of their lives for having saved them; and too many of those who learned to kill as a highly valued and rewarded activity, then come home to be severely punished for minor infractions of the law.

We have invented drugs to promote sleep, eliminate physical pain and anxiety, and have created uncounted thousands of drug addicts, to say nothing of crippled thalidomide babies.

It is time we began to realize that no matter what we have achieved intellectually, human beings cannot adapt to the overwhelming contradictions which characterize their daily lives without serious impairment of their emotional health and functioning. Our scientific knowledge increases day by day with unbelievable rapidity. What will come of it in the next decade or two dwarfs the imagination. Within twenty years, according to some predictions, two percent of human beings would be able to do all the necessary work of the world. What would the others do?

Before it is too late, we must awaken to

the fact that if we continue to use the achievements of intellect to isolate human beings from one another and to force them into physical, emotional and intellectual passivity, their aggressive drive—denied all healthy expression—will mobilize their destructiveness to a terrifying degree. This, combined with our ever-increasing manipulation of the forces of nature will lead to destruction unparalleled in the violence-filled history of man.

If we are to reverse this trend, we must begin by utilizing what we have learned about the true nature of the human animal. If we are to survive, we must first of all come to understand who and what we really are, not what we wish or pretend to be. Only then will there be hope for change, will we be able to use the fruits of our intellect for our benefit, not for our annihilation.

Psychoanalysis does not claim to have all the answers to the evils which beset humanity, but whatever it can teach us about the true nature of man, his basic drives and emotional needs, should help us to understand and to reverse the dangerous course upon which we are embarked. Psychoanalysis has been widely misunderstood and distorted from its inception. It is my hope that this effort to clarify its meaning and to obviate the misconceptions surrounding it will be useful.

# Appendix

THE AMERICAN PSYCHOANALYTIC
ASSOCIATION
1 East 57th Street, New York, N. Y. 10022

*AFFILIATED SOCIETIES OF AMERICAN
PSYCHOANALYTIC ASSOCIATION
1967–1968*

ASSOCIATION FOR PSYCHOANALYTIC MEDI-
CINE (NEW YORK)
1025 Fifth Avenue, New York, N. Y. 10028

BALTIMORE PSYCHOANALYTIC SOCIETY
821 No. Charles St., Baltimore, Md. 21201

BOSTON PSYCHOANALYTIC SOCIETY & INSTI-
TUTE, INC.
15 Commonwealth Ave., Boston, Mass. 02116

CHICAGO PSYCHOANALYTIC SOCIETY
670 No. Michigan Ave., Chicago, Ill. 60611

CINCINNATI PSYCHOANALYTIC SOCIETY
Dept. of Psychiatry, Cincinnati General Hospital
Cincinnati, Ohio 45229

CLEVELAND PSYCHOANALYTIC SOCIETY
Benjamin Rose Hospital, 2073 Abingdon Road
Cleveland, Ohio

DENVER PSYCHOANALYTIC SOCIETY
4200 E. 9th Ave., Denver, Colo. 80220

DETROIT PSYCHOANALYTIC SOCIETY
17595 Parkside, Detroit, Mich. 48221

FLORIDA PSYCHOANALYTIC SOCIETY
4950 Lejeune Road
Coral Gables, Florida 33146

LONG ISLAND PSYCHOANALYTIC SOCIETY
23 The Hemlocks
Roslyn Estates, New York 11576

LOS ANGELES PSYCHOANALYTIC SOCIETY
344 No. Bedford Drive, Beverly Hills, Calif. 90210

MICHIGAN ASSOCIATION FOR PSYCHOANALY-
SIS
18466 Wildmere Ave., Detroit, Mich. 48221

MICHIGAN PSYCHOANALYTIC SOCIETY
505 New Center Bldg., Detroit, Mich. 48202

NEW JERSEY PSYCHOANALYTIC SOCIETY
301 Broad Ave., Englewood, N. J. 07631

NEW ORLEANS PSYCHOANALYTIC SOCIETY
3624 Coliseum St., New Orleans, La. 70115

NEW YORK PSYCHOANALYTIC SOCIETY
247 East 82d St., New York, N. Y. 10028

PHILADELPHIA ASSN. FOR PSYCHOANALYSIS
111 No. 49th St., Philadelphia, Pa. 19139

PHILADELPHIA PSYCHOANALYTIC SOCIETY,
INC.
Beekman Place, Suite 422
2747 Belmont Ave., Philadelphia, Pa. 19131

PITTSBURGH PSYCHOANALYTIC SOCIETY
3811 O'Hara St., Pittsburgh, Pa. 15213

PSYCHOANALYTIC ASSN. OF NEW YORK, INC.
11 Fifth Ave., New York, N. Y. 10003

SAN FRANCISCO PSYCHOANALYTIC SOCIETY
2420 Sutter St., San Francisco, Calif. 94115

SEATTLE PSYCHOANALYTIC SOCIETY
2271 No. East 51st St., Seattle, Wash. 98105

SOUTHERN CALIFORNIA PSYCHOANALYTIC
SOCIETY
9024 West Olympic Blvd., Beverly Hills, Calif. 90211

TOPEKA PSYCHOANALYTIC SOCIETY
3617 W. Sixth Ave., Box 829, Topeka, Kansas 66601

WASHINGTON PSYCHOANALYTIC SOCIETY
4925 MacArthur Blvd. N.W., Washington, D.C. 20007

WESTCHESTER PSYCHOANALYTIC SOCIETY
80 Summit Drive, Hastings-on-Hudson, N. Y. 10706

WESTERN NEW ENGLAND PSYCHOANALYTIC
SOCIETY
759 Chestnut St., Springfield, Mass. 01107

WESTERN NEW YORK PSYCHOANALYTIC
SOCIETY
261 Alexander St., Rochester, N. Y. 14607

# Index